THE ASPHALT WARRIOR

GARY REILLY

RUNNING METER PRESS
DENVER

PUBLISHED BY
Running Meter Press
2509 Xanthia Street, Denver, CO 80238
Publisher@RunningMeterPress.com
720 328 5488

COVER ART by John Sherfflius
COVER AND TEXT DESIGN by Nick Zelinger, www.nzgraphics.com

ISBN: 978-0-9847860-0-8
LIBRARY OF CONGRESS CONTROL NUMBER: 2011942108

First Edition 2012
Printed in the United States of America

FOREWORD

Allow me to introduce Denverite Brendan Murphy, or "Murph" as he's known to the rest of the world. That world consists mostly of fares and doormen and fellow hacks from the Rocky Mountain Taxicab Company. He lives alone in his crow's nest of an apartment, fries a hamburger for every meal, does his dish, then channel surfs for reruns of *Gilligan's Island*.

To Murph, the mystery of the universe can be reduced to a single question: "Why would anyone want to DO anything?" (Besides produce a trunkful of unpublishable novels.)

But despite his radical minimalism and aversion to lifting a finger, Murph somehow gets entangled in the messy lives of his passengers. Why? Irish-Catholic guilt, perhaps. A headful of his dear ma's rules of life, maybe. Or, it just might be that the guy has a big heart.

Murph is the fictional creation of Gary Reilly, a man who shared many of Murph's qualities.

Reilly's alter ego first appeared as an advice columnist on AOL in the mid-1990s. Readers would step into his virtual taxi to spill their guts and Murph would dispense his quirky brand of wisdom. Happy correspondents often left imaginary tips for their iconoclastic driver. In a two-year run, the wildly popular Murph generated close to a million words of dialog with his passengers.

When that gig ended, Reilly transferred Murph from the digital realm to the page. *The Asphalt Warrior* is the first of ten Murph novels.

Reilly, like his literary counterpart, was dedicated to the art and craft of fiction. Besides the Murph series, Gary wrote ten more novels, some based on his experiences as a Vietnam vet. While his strength was humor, he was equally adept at searing and serious prose.

Early on, one of his short stories, "The Biography Man," appeared in the prestigious 1977 Pushcart Prize Winners collection. As he moved to longer forms of fiction, he was in no hurry to be published. Instead, he poured his energy into editing previous work and starting new projects.

He served as a mentor and writing coach for aspiring authors, some who have made the local best-seller lists. He created a manuscript on the plotting of novels, which included a clear paradigm along with detailed analyses of twenty modern classics.

It wasn't until about two years ago that Gary decided it was time to get his books out to the public. He began with query letters to New York agents. As he expected, the process was slow, the pipeline long. He began to explore other options: smaller presses, print-on-demand, electronic media.

But Gary ran out of time. On March 10, 2011, lovers of good fiction lost a star they'd never known.

Now, with the support of his family, long-time partner Sherry Peterson, and novelist Mark Stevens, Murph lives.

We've all climbed into cabs driven by outcasts, met oddball characters in fiction, and gotten an earful of advice from unexpected quarters. But, at least for me, I have yet to meet anybody quite like this asphalt warrior.

Go ahead, hop in. Let Murph take you for a ride.

—MIKE KEEFE
January 2012

CHAPTER 1

I was first in line at the cabstand outside the Hilton Hotel in downtown Denver when a nervous man in his thirties hopped into the backseat of my taxi. I was immediately annoyed because the man hadn't come out of the hotel. He was what I call a "pedestrian," and pedestrians rarely want to go to Denver International Airport. I don't know who they were, but I love the masters of inconvenience who thought up DIA. They placed it twenty-five miles northeast of town.

"Where to?" I said.

"I'm not sure," the man replied.

I twisted around in my seat to examine him. This is a technique cab drivers employ to avoid getting robbed. The fact that I have never been robbed does not validate the hypothesis, although I like to think it does. Self-delusion is better than Valium when you're trapped inside a taxi with a madman, and a lot cheaper. But the man was wearing an expensive overcoat, a white shirt, and a classy tie. This was a relief. He looked employed. A lot of men who get into my cab look like me.

"What do you mean you're not sure?" I said, buying time. I glanced at Francois. He's the doorman at the Hilton. Sometimes doormen are your only hope in a dicey situation. They have phones at their posts. They can have the cops swarming all over your taxi before your fare has time to reload.

"My wife was supposed to meet me here," the man said. He glanced out the rear window. "We had a lunch date at Biloxi's."

I calmed down. Biloxi's is a swank restaurant in the Cherry Creek Shopping Center. A seven-dollar trip plus a three-dollar tip, practically guaranteed. Cheapskates never dine at Biloxi's.

"So ... do you want me to run you over to Biloxi's?" I said.

He licked his lips and swallowed hard. "Would it be okay if we waited here for a few minutes? She might show up."

I debated whether or not to act exasperated. The man looked like a potential big tipper, but time is money in the taxi business, so rather than pretend to be exasperated, I decided to lie. "Public Utilities Commission rules require me to run the meter if we wait," I said.

That wasn't a PUC rule, that was my rule, but people are rarely impressed by my rules.

He reached inside his coat. I wondered if he was going for a pistol tucked into a shoulder-holster. That's because I've seen too many cop shows. When I was growing up my Maw told me that television destroys the imagination, but TV has given me an imagination you couldn't buy in an opium den.

The man pulled out a billfold. His hands were trembling. "That's all right," he said. "I'll pay you for the waiting time."

"You don't have to pay me in advance," I said, surprising myself. I had never said those words before in my life. "I'll just pull ahead and we'll wait."

I started the engine, dropped the shift into low, idled forward past the entryway of the Hilton, and parked farther along the curb. The cabs behind me pulled forward one space. The engines shut down. A stillness swept the street. It was another listless summer day in Denver.

We waited. The man kept glancing out the back window. As I watched him in my rear-view mirror I ran through my mental Rolodex of small-talk, debating whether or not to strike up a conversation. Silence in a cab can be unnerving. But the guy seemed distracted, which was okay with me. I would just as soon never converse with any of my fares, but that's not the way the taxi game is played.

I was surprised at how quickly I became adept at small-talk fourteen years ago when I first started hacking. After I became a cabbie I discovered that it was like being an actor. I discovered that behind the wheel of a cab I fell into a certain role depending on the personality of my customer. I realized that people expected me to be someone I wasn't—a cabbie. They expected me to be streetwise and hip to things the average Joe didn't know. I was a Hollywood cliché to them, I was a cardboard cut-out, I wasn't me. I liked that. People paid me to be a fraud. It was a dream come true.

The man continued to look out the rear window for a bit, then he turned back with a sigh. "I guess she's not coming," he said.

"Do you want me to run you over to Biloxi's?" I said again. He glanced at my eyes in the mirror with a querulous expression, as if surprised to find me sitting three feet away from him. He began chewing his lower lip.

I figured he was going to bail out on me and I would have to pull back to the rear of the line at the cabstand. But you get used to situations like this when you hack for a living. Who knows? Maybe my next fare would be going to Aspen. By getting shuffled around in the cab line you sometimes ended up scoring big. It does happen, believe me. Hacking is a gamble, a roll of the dice, a deal of the cards, a yank on a one-armed bandit. It took me a long time to get used to the idea that all of my fears are as unrealistic as all of my hopes.

"Who does your hair?" the man said. I froze.

"My hair?"

"Pardon me for asking," he said, "but I'm a barber. I was just curious. You have a ... unique ... hairstyle."

I turned around in my seat. "I cut my own hair."

I was sporting long, bushy hair at the time. Long hair was part of my cabbie persona. I usually combed my shag over my face and then cut off everything I could see—quick and easy, down and dirty. That's how I live, that's how I love, that's how I practice personal hygiene.

The man reached inside his coat and pulled out a card and handed it to me. "I'm sorry, but I guess my wife isn't going to show up," he said. "How about if I give you ten dollars, and here's my card. Why don't you drop by sometime and I'll give you a free haircut just to make up for putting you to all this trouble."

The card read: Gino's Barbershop.

I chuckled inwardly. This had been about as much trouble as changing channels with a TV remote. But I had to put on an act for him because he was being apologetic. I liked that. It made me feel "special." You don't get too many opportunities to feel special when you drive a taxi, so I decided to milk it. I reached up and took the card and the money. "Gosh, thanks mister," I said, falling into my most obsequious posture. I have a wide range of postures. The size, contour, and emotional characteristic of each posture is governed by tips.

"My wife must have been delayed by some other business," he said as he gathered himself together and climbed out of the cab.

"No problem, sir," I said. "And thanks for the haircut."

He shut the door and walked quickly back the way he had come. I watched him in my rear-view mirror as he strode down the sidewalk, then I looked at the card in my hand. A barber. I started to tear the card in two. But then something inside me told me to keep it. Something having to do with the way I was brought up by my Maw. Something having to do with getting things for free.

I slipped the card into my plastic briefcase and started the engine. I was ten bucks to the good and I hadn't driven anywhere. The day was turning out okay.

I cruised around the block and pulled back into line, shut off my engine, turned on the AM radio ... *myyy ba-bee does the hanky-panky* ... shut it off and commenced to reading a paperback. I possessed something like peace of mind. It was June, it was a late Monday afternoon, the street in front of the Hilton was quiet, and I had at least a half hour to read my book.

And then the dream died.

People started coming out of the Hilton, accompanied by porters hugging suitcases. I cursed my luck. As much as I like money, I like doing nothing even better, which was why I had stuck with cab driving for fourteen years. I had once held a job as a white-collar worker for the Dyna-Plex Corporation down in the Denver Tech Center and I never did any work at all. I had gotten plenty used to it. But the problem with Dyna-Plex was that you had to pretend to be working when you sat at your desk, and as far as I was concerned that was taking fraud just a little too far.

A porter approached my taxi before I could even pull forward in line. Sudden eruptions from hotels are fairly common. One minute you're in

Tahiti and the next minute it's Tarawa. I hopped out of my cab and opened the trunk. The porter tossed in four bags, then opened my rear door for a little old lady. I ran back and hopped into the driver's seat and started the engine just as a stream of taxis came squealing around the corner. The Word was out. The hotel was jumping and so was the radio: "L-5 Hilton!" meaning the hotel needed taxis. I had lucked out by being in line prior to the deluge. Five minutes from now there would be seven cabbies in line grinding their teeth with frustration because the show would be over and the Hilton would be dead.

"Would you please take me to the airport?" the lady said.

My heart soared like an eagle. A fifty-buck trip out of the blue, from the Hilton to DIA.

I would be quitting early today.

"Yes, ma'am, and how are you?" I said, dropping my red flag and turning on the meter.

"I'm fine, but I have a niece who's going in for an operation." Little old ladies' nieces were always going in for operations. I spun my mental Rolodex and stopped at S for Sympathy.

"I'm sorry to hear that, ma'am," I said. "What is the nature of your niece's affliction?" She gave me a brief rundown, and then I got a detailed description of a gallbladder operation that she herself had undergone when she was somebody's niece.

After I dropped the woman off at DIA I took a moment to tote my loot. I was up seventy bucks for the day, clear profit. A little bell went off inside my head, the closing bell—last call. I eased the shift into third gear and began cruising back toward Denver, the Mile-High City, the municipality which, for legal reasons, I am forced to refer to as my "current place of residence."

Let me tell you a little bit about myself. I was born in Wichita, Kansas. That covers my childhood.

After I got out of the army I spent my first two years of college in Kansas being a mile high, so when I came to Denver I knew I had found a home. And when I landed this cab-driving gig, I knew I had found The

Answer. I had lived in a lot of places, punched a lot of time clocks and collected a lot of unemployment checks before I went to work for the Rocky Mountain Taxicab Company (RMTC). I learned that you'll never get rich driving a cab but you can stay out of debt. I've been broke, and I've been in debt, and broke is better.

I arrived back in the city a half hour later and fought the urge to take one more call off the radio and pick up one more sawbuck before turning in my cab. It's like I said: cab driving is like yanking the handle on a one-armed bandit. It can get addictive. The flow of money is endless because people are always going somewhere. But I had learned long ago to stop asking the most baffling philosophical question of all time: Why would anybody go anywhere?

CHAPTER 2

I drove back to Rocky Cab, which is located near the Interstate 70 viaduct north of downtown Denver. I parked in the dirt lot and went into the on-call room where I turned in my key and trip-sheet. The room was filled with cab drivers sitting at tables waiting for their assigned vehicles to come in off the road for the night shift but I didn't hang around to shoot the bull with any of them. Call me a curmudgeon but I never shoot the bull with cab drivers. I don't even talk to them. As far as I know, none of them like me, which is the way I like it. But there is one driver who talks to me fairly regularly. His name is Big Al.

As my mentor, as the man who had put me through my paces when I was in training to become an asphalt warrior fourteen years ago, he seemed to have taken a special interest in my case, in the way that a university professor might take a special interest in the education of a young man who shows signs of genius. That's one way of looking at it. Another way of looking at it is a professor who takes a special interest in a student who is so hopeless that only intense tutoring will help him to avoid expulsion. I'll let you be the judge.

I walked out of the on-call room and drove to my apartment building, which is located on Capitol Hill. I parked in the dirt lot behind my building, got out of my Chevy and climbed the rear fire escape to the door on my third floor apartment. It opens to the kitchen, which is like a big box that was added on to the top floor after the building was converted from a rich man's mansion to an apartment building, probably during the Depression years. I suspect it was once the maid's quarters.

I stood in the kitchen and opened my plastic briefcase and pulled out my cash. The barber's business card dropped onto the table. I glanced at it, then counted my money. I went into the living room and hid the profits in my copy of *Finnegans Wake*, the one book I knew would never be stolen from my apartment.

I went back into the kitchen and glanced at the card lying on the table. "Gino's." The barbershop was located on east Colfax Avenue, almost in Aurora—the gateway to Kansas. Was the man who had been inside my taxi Gino himself, or was he one of Gino's employees? I figured I would never find out.

I picked up the card and looked it over, wondering why anyone in his right mind would give away a free haircut. I'm wary of the word "free," as in "free sample" or "free will." What's the catch?

Then I caught a look at myself in the reflection of my toaster. I sighed, and walked over to the cork bulletin board hanging on the wall. I pinned the card next to a free pass to Putt-Putt Golf that I had been hauling around since I was fourteen years old. Some dreams never die.

I opened the refrigerator, and pulled out a hamburger patty. I had recently made a discovery that changed my life. I had found that it was possible to buy hamburger patties already shaped like big dots. They were in the meat department at the grocery store, stocked in an obscure section where I had never gone before because it was where the expensive meats were sold. But I happened to be pushing my shopping cart down the aisle where they sell fresh fish. I have never bought a fish in my life. As I trudged along I started glancing sideways at the expensive meats the way a poor person might glance surreptitiously at diamond necklaces in a Tiffany's window. Then I noticed these big white dots.

It turned out that they were pre-shaped hamburger patties separated by circular sheets of waxed paper, which tossed me for a loop because when I was a little kid my Maw had shaped hamburgers by hand, and she subsequently taught me how to shape hamburgers when I was in college. To put it another way, she forced me to shape my own hamburgers because she was "fed up with waiting on yer royal highness hand and foot." It was a good thing she got fed up because shaping hamburger patties by hand is not the kind of thing you want to learn through trial and error. To draw a parallel, I once tried to boil a chicken in a pan of Mazola.

I slapped a fresh patty onto the frying pan and listened to the sizzle of the meat. Pre-shaped meat sizzles differently from hand-molded meat. It has a uniform sizzle. The patties I molded by hand were kind of lumpy, so they had a different sound because not all of the meat was touching the bottom of the frying pan at the same time, which meant I had to flatten the meat with a spatula. This worked, but it was a crude method of getting all the meat to touch the heated metal, and the sound was chaotic. But the pre-shaped patties had a nice even tone. I stood at the stove listening to the uniform sizzle, but then something strange came over me. I started to feel sort of useless. I had an itch to flatten the patty, even though it couldn't have been flatter because it had been made by a machine, probably one with a blade honed to razor sharpness.

Fortunately I still had to scoop the patty up with the spatula and flip it over, so I didn't feel totally useless. But then out of habit I accidentally pressed the spatula against the meat and ruined the perfectly flat surface. It made a rectangular indent. I gritted my teeth with remorse because I knew that when I flipped the patty back over, all of the meat wouldn't be touching the bottom of the pan. There would be a small rectangular section, like the roof of a cave made of meat that wouldn't be touching the metal, so the sound of the sizzle would be different. It would sound like a nun chastising me for misspelling a word.

I tried not to think about it.

When the burger was cooked I slapped it onto a bun and went into the living room. I switched on the TV and channel-surfed while I ate. I stopped at *Gilligan's Island*. The Skipper was yelling at Gilligan. I didn't blame him. No phones, no lights, no motorboats, not a single luxury, except Ginger and Mary Ann. Mary Ann was from Winfield, Kansas, according to the producer, Sherwood Schwartz. Eugene Pallette was from Winfield, too. He had a voice like a frog and played Friar Tuck in *The Adventures of Robin Hood* (1938). I drove through Winfield one night eighteen years ago. I

didn't stop to look around. It's like they say in Kansas—if you've seen New-
ton, you've seen Winfield.

Mary Ann is my favorite castaway. As I stood there watching the TV,
I debated whether or not to wait for her to come onstage. They don't make
short-shorts like those anymore. But I gave up and turned off the TV and
went into the kitchen to do the dish. Then I stepped into the bathroom.

I stared at my face in the mirror. Then I stared at my hair.

I opened the medicine cabinet, eyeballed the razor blades like I always do,
then pulled out a small pair of silver barber shears that had been left behind
in my cab five years earlier. People are always leaving things in the backseat of
my taxi. I could furnish Barbie's Dream House with all the loot I have "taken
into protective custody." Know anybody who wants to buy a lava lamp?

I closed the medicine cabinet, picked up my hairbrush, and began
sweeping my shaggy mane up from the back of my head and down across
my eyes. Everything went black. I parted the hair in the middle, grabbed a
hunk, and raised the shears. But suddenly I couldn't do it. Who was I kidding? Somewhere on the mean streets of Denver, a haircut was waiting for
me. If I trimmed my hair now, the barber would catch on and I subsequently would be embarrassed. I hate being embarrassed. It gets old.

I set the shears down, went into the kitchen and grabbed a beer. I
walked into the living room and flopped down on my easy chair and began
channel-surfing, but my heart wasn't in it. I was torn between the idea of
getting a haircut as well as not paying for it. Which was better?

I started to feel edgy. Decisions do that to me. It made sense that a
barber would say something about shaggy hair in general, but whenever
anybody "says something" about any part of my body, I develop a psychological tic. That doesn't include my beer belly. I laugh when people remark
on my beer belly. I really need some kind of goddamn therapy. When I
worked for Dyna-Plex, I got my hair cut once a week. Okay. I'll admit it.
I got it "styled." Two days before I started work I went to a men's salon for
a complete makeover from the hairline up.

On the day that I applied for the job as a corporate writer I brought
along my English diploma. I had heard on the street that corporations pre-

ferred to hire people with college degrees. I didn't believe a word of it because I didn't place any value on college degrees—the fact that I had one proved how much they were worth. But the fact that I didn't believe corporations were impressed by college degrees indicated that I was wrong about corporations. My inability to interpret reality correctly has stood me in good stead over the years.

I borrowed a two-piece suit from an old college friend named Wally who had a real job. I promised to get it back to him in two pieces by five the next afternoon. I didn't want to buy a suit unless I got hired. I couldn't think of anything more annoying than having a useless suit hanging in my closet. I already had a pair of twenty pound dumbbells gathering dust in there. Also a ThighMaster.

But Wally's wife didn't want him to loan me the suit. His wife didn't like me. She thought I was a bad influence on him. This was a conclusion wrought by deductive logic on her part. Her evidence was collected at a kegger during one particular spring break in college where I was given the nickname "Howling Wolf" by the attendees. They took a vote. The vote was between two potential nicknames: "Howling Wolf" and "The Dork." The rest of the kegger story is long and complicated and funny to men, so let's drop it. Wally did loan me the suit though. Most of my married friends don't pay much attention to what their wives hate.

On the following Monday I made an attempt at combing my shag before I went in for the Dyna-Plex interview, so it was sort of flat. "Sort of flat" is as good a description as any, and better than most. The vice president who interviewed me for the job was only thirty-five years old. But I knew I wasn't going to get the job the moment I walked into his office with my flat hair, my ill-fitting suit, and my English diploma dangling from my fingertips. The vice president looked like a male model. But I think I intrigued him. The ten other job applicants seated in the waiting room were dressed like conventional office workers. To draw an analogy, it was like the difference between ten Norman Rockwell paintings and a Jackson Pollock.

The VP offered me a seat and stared at my hair while I explained my checkered past. After I had fully accepted the idea that my being hired for a white-collar job was a concept that extended beyond the bounds of rational thought, I mentioned to him that I once got lost in Wichita while streaking. This was at another kegger. It's a long story so I don't want to go into it, but he did. This led to further descriptions of other things that had happened to me between the ages of nineteen and twenty-seven, including the "Howling Wolf" vote, and the next thing I knew he was calling the human resources director in to finish the hiring process.

See?

I was wrong.

I knew I wasn't going to get the job, and I got it. As evidential counterpoint to my "Theory of Wrongness" I have been convinced for the past fourteen years that I am going to win the Colorado State Lottery and I haven't won it yet.

After I filled out the hiring paperwork, the VP got serious and told me that I would have to get a haircut before I showed up for work on the first day. He apologized but said that the CEO would fire me if I came to work on Monday morning looking "the way you do now." This made me bristle. I was young. I was rebellious. My attitude was: I look the way I look because that's who I really am and I have no intention of pretending to be someone I'm not. This was back in the days when I thought honesty was a virtue and not a strategic error. But I was broke, so when he told me that my starting salary would be twenty thousand dollars a year I asked him if he knew a good barber.

Ergo, the "salon."

I got my hair styled before I returned the suit to Wally. He did not recognize me when he opened his front door. My hair was trimmed and parted in the middle. I had to reintroduce myself to a guy I had known for three years in college. He stared at me for a long time, then he said, "You look like your sister."

His wife came to the door scowling as usual, but when she saw me, her expression changed. For one moment I thought she was going to start liking me. I was wrong. But her face began trembling with what I recognized as suppressed laughter. I ignored this as I returned the suit. I don't know which is worse, being despised or laughed at by women—but maybe they're the same thing.

I lasted only a year at Dyna-Plex. The vice president lost his job one month after hiring me, but I cannot say that there was a link between his dismissal and my arrival. That would fall into the category of "The Generic Fallacy." After all, if you sneeze at the same moment the electricity goes out, that does not mean you caused it, unless you were trying to fix the toaster. My Maw made me buy her a new toaster, as well as a new fork.

Anyway, as I sat there in my crow's nest that night, the word "free" kept buzzing around my face like a mosquito. I finally did what I always do when faced with a difficult decision. I went into my bedroom, turned off the lights, and collapsed into bed.

CHAPTER 3

"The supervisor wants to see you." It was Wednesday morning. I was standing in the on-call room at Rocky Cab, waiting for the man to give me my taxi key and my trip-sheet. His name was Rollo. Aside from a thick Plexiglass window, the only thing that stood between Rollo and me was antipathy.

"What's it about?" I said.

Rollo's lips formed something resembling a smile. It was a pinched smile, the kind you might see on the face of Victor Buono, one of the most underrated actors who ever took pleasure in other people's discomfort. He lifted a donut from a saucer and took a slow bite. He shrugged and said between chews, "All I know is what they told me upstairs. Hogan wants to talk to you." I reached for my key and trip-sheet, but Rollo shook his head no. I got the message. No cab until I talked to my supervisor. I walked into the hallway, climbed the narrow staircase that led up to the head office, and knocked on the door.

Hogan said, "Yeah," in the same sullen tone of voice that a juvenile delinquent says "Yuh" when a high school counselor asks if he's going to buckle down and study harder.

I pushed the door open and walked in.

I don't know Hogan's first name. Don't want to know it. I learned his last name the day I applied for my job as a cab driver. During the following years I had learned the names of his spies who would report you if you committed an infraction of Rocky Cab rules while on duty, such as curb hopping, rolling stops, or short-changing blind men—the kind of things cops frown on, too. It had been thirteen years since I had short-changed a blind man, but I didn't do it on purpose. It's a long story. Let's drop it.

Hogan was seated behind his desk, leafing through a manila folder. The lenses of his eyeglasses are as thick as the bottoms of pop bottles. They press the flesh of his cheeks down to his sagging chin. Over the past fourteen years I have stood witness to the collapse of his face.

"Thanks for coming up, Murph," he said. "I've been looking through the records. It's time for your annual physical. Why don't you run over to the DOT clinic sometime this week and get your checkup, okay?"

I swallowed hard. I nodded. I hated getting naked in front of another man, even if he was a doctor. The Department of Transportation clinic was housed in a building over near the old Stapleton Airport site in east Denver, not far from where the blind man lived.

"Sure thing," I said.

Meeting over.

By the time I got downstairs, Hogan had informed Rollo via intercom that I was cleared for duty. Rollo gave me a querulous look with his eyebrows raised. I debated whether or not to tell him the upshot of the meeting.

The problem is that the man in the cage is a power center at a taxi company. He can prevent a cabbie from going on duty under certain circumstances, especially if you look unfit for driving, which I sometimes do, usually when I come to work. You don't want to hassle the man in the cage.

"Time for my physical," I said.

Rollo gave me a supercilious smile and held out my key and trip-sheet.

I smiled and said, "Thanks," jerk.

My cab once did time as a police interceptor for the Denver Police Department, but now it was just Rocky Mountain Taxicab Company Vehicle #127, refurbished and painted wintergreen by the boys in the garage. When something goes wrong, as it inevitably does to an automobile that has more than four hundred thousand miles under its hood, a tow truck hauls it into the shop and the boys go to work. They're magicians. Down time never lasts more than an hour before I'm back on the road. You don't want to hassle mechanics, either. I don't want to imply that there are people in this world whom you do want to hassle, although telephone solicitors come to mind.

I pulled first-echelon maintenance on 127, checked the oil, water, and transmission levels, kicked the tires, and looked for dents. I share 127 with other drivers, sometimes acquaintances, sometimes strangers, and sometimes the worst strangers of all: newbies. Having been a newbie myself fourteen years ago, I know how inept newbies can be—I wrote the book. Apparently a lot of newbies have read my book, but I didn't find any dents or dings that morning. I climbed into the driver's seat and started the engine.

I drove to the nearest 7-11 to gas up and buy a cup of coffee and a Twinkie. I didn't rush. I had to go take my physical later in the day, and the thought of doing something other than sitting in the driver's seat of 127 drained me of energy and ambition. Most thoughts do that to me.

To counter my mild depression I put myself into a state of mind that I call "cabbie consciousness." It's sort of like Transcendental Meditation but doesn't involve a mantra. It's more like watching television. I pretend that whatever I'm doing at the current moment in time is valid, as opposed to what I should be doing, which is rushing to buy gas, picking up fares, making up for the time I would lose by taking the physical, and generally acting mature and responsible.

Give me a break.

I arrived at 7-11 but had to wait five minutes for a line of cars at the gas pump. This shattered my calm. The 7-11 where I gas up is located at what you might call "the edge of the city," which is in north Denver near the viaducts. Most people are afraid to get out of their cars in that part of town. There's something about viaducts that give people the willies. But elevated roadways don't bother me. I just keep my back to them and concentrate on squeezing out the unleaded. I do keep my eyes closed but that's because the fumes make my whites red and I have found that red-eyed cab drivers give fares the willies.

After I hung up the pump I strolled into the 7-11. And froze.

There were fifteen customers standing in line. I looked outside. Maybe three cars parked in the lot. Where the hell did all these time-destroyers come from? I rushed to the coffee machine and filled a paper cup, then snatched a Twinkie and raced to the end of the line before anybody else magically appeared out of nowhere. There's nothing that infuriates me more than a long line at 7-11. Losing my TV remote runs a close second, so you can imagine how I felt that morning.

Then I did something I almost never do. I glanced at my wristwatch. I hate time in general and clocks in particular, but I had learned that a cab driver has to own a watch. This relates to picking up fares on time. Need I say more? But I sure as hell never looked at a wristwatch while buying a Twinkie. The whole scene left a sour taste in my mouth. I almost put the Twinkie back.

I didn't recognize the clerk. He looked like a newbie. Young. Nervous. Trying to deal with the process of selling a money order to an old lady. The old lady was counting out pennies from a change purse.

I nearly collapsed mentally. My gas tank was full so I couldn't put the unleaded back on the shelf and flee. I was trapped. Everybody else in line was holding chips and candy bars and bottled water. They could have said to hell with it and put their items back on the shelves and walked out. So why didn't they?

I did my best to encourage them. I began sighing with impatience. It didn't work. Each customer had staked out his private square of tile and was standing firm, waiting for the old lady to get the exact change right down to the last corroded Lincoln head. Old ladies do this in order to "help" clerks. Thank God taximeters round off to twenty cents. It reduces my mental collapses by a factor of five.

I won't describe the time-destruction engaged in by the customers ahead of me. I won't do to you what they did to me. Let's just say it was a quarter till eight before I got back into my cab, took a sip of cold coffee, and vowed that as long as I lived I would never again fill my gas tank without scouting the terrain for enemy presence. Fortunately, I knew how to do this. I once saw an army training film.

I placed the dead joe in my cupholder, then started the engine and pulled away from the 7-11. It made me feel bad to have ill feelings toward my favorite store. I'm old enough to remember when 7-11 stores actually opened at 7 and closed at 11, and believe me, brother, that was a quantum leap in the evolution of Denver. It made me feel like I possessed an embarrassment of riches every time I strolled into a 7-11 at 10:55 to buy a pack of smokes. I was taken down a peg when I visited my evil brother Gavin in California and discovered that liquor stores—not bars but liquor stores—stayed open past two A.M. That's when I realized Albert Einstein was wrong. "Relativity" wasn't the right word. "Pathos" nailed it. But I came back to Denver anyway. Apartment prices here were peanuts relative to the West Coast.

As I drove away from the 7-11, I saw a man waving frantically to me. He was standing on a corner where a small park was located. No shops or stores or even houses nearby. He was a pedestrian. Normally I never pick up pedestrians who try to flag me down. It's a safety thing. Cabbies sometimes get robbed by people who don't phone the RMTC dispatcher for a ride. If you pick someone up off the street, the company has no idea that you've got a fare in your backseat, which is how robbers like it.

But I was behind schedule and I hadn't made a dime, so I literally heaved a sigh of resignation and pulled over to the curb. I figured I was safe. He looked okay. Well-dressed. Mid-thirties. Nicely groomed. Ted Bundy looked that way when he escaped from the Aspen jail.

The pedestrian leaned into my window. "I'm only going a few blocks but I missed my bus and I'm late for work. Can you take me there?" He named the address.

"Climb in," I said. A three-dollar ride at best. It didn't matter. I was going in that direction anyway. Three bucks is three bucks said John Jacob Astor probably.

A couple minutes later I pulled over to the curb. The guy handed me a twenty.

I looked at it.

Then I looked at the meter. Three bucks.

Suddenly three bucks wasn't three bucks. It was Mount St. Helens. "Do you have anything smaller than this?" I said. I had only twenty dollars worth of change on me.

"No, I don't," he said, with panic in his eyes.

My instinct was to give him the ride for free, but I dug into my starting change and handed him seventeen dollar bills.

Did he tip me?

I won't bore you with the answer.

After he hurried away I drove down the block holding the twenty in my right hand, which was resting against the steering wheel at the two o'clock position. I glanced at Andrew Jackson's face. Ol' Andy Jackson, seventh president of the United States. A nun made us memorize the presidents back in sixth grade, so I knew our forefathers numerically. That was the only instance during my grade school years when I was good at math. But I had a secret. I didn't memorize the numbers, I memorized the words, i.e., "seven" rather than "7." Keep that under your hat.

Allow me to mention here that Andrew Jackson is not to be confused with Thomas "Stonewall" Jackson who commanded the "Rebs" at Bull Run. I used to do that all the time. Not command "Rebs," but get confused.

Well, here I was once again unable to proceed with my life until I did something with money. I had a full tank of gas and a twenty-dollar bill in my hand, yet I couldn't pick up any fares until I turned the bill into small change. O. Henry could have done wonders with that premise.

I drove past a car wash and slowed down because car washes have change machines. But then I stepped on the gas and kept driving. Just the thought of stuffing my last twenty down the gullet of a machine that promised to give me change made me laugh out loud. I'm onto you, O. Henry.

Instead I drove to a Starbucks and bought a fresh cup of mocha. I'm not even going to apologize for that. I sure didn't apologize to the clerk for handing him a twenty so early in the morning. I figured a store that sells nothing but coffee would have plenty of change. I'll admit it. I occasionally like to have a slug of yuppie mud with all its fancy frills. I'll take my alkaloid diuretics wherever I can get them. If there isn't a 7-11 in the vicinity, a Winchell's donut shop is Plan B. The joe at both places is almost indistinguishable, like the difference between Johnny Walker and Cutty Sark, but only cab drivers and hobos draw such fine distinctions.

It was eight-fifteen when I finally turned on my RMTC radio and started listening to the dispatcher yelling at the newbies. I did not head for a hotel. I normally park at the cabstand at the Brown Palace in downtown Denver at dawn and read paperbacks until a fare climbs into the backseat and says, "DIA." But that plan was down the crapper. I had to actually work that day. Taking calls off the radio is how a real cab driver makes money. He doesn't sit in front of hotels and he doesn't sit out at the airport. He takes radio calls one right after another. The fact that I'm a real cab driver does not invalidate the hypothesis. I know I'm a real cab driver because I have a license. I do sit in front of hotels but I never sit out at the airport. On the surface this might indicate that I am only half a real cab driver, or else half a phony. Take your pick. All I know is that every April 15th I write "Taxi Driver" on my 1040 and not "Phony."

I turned the volume up on the radio and began listening to calls, or "bells" as we say in cabbie lingo. "Motor" is another bit of taxi jargon. It refers to the cab company itself. When the dispatcher tells you to return to the motor, he means come back to headquarters because Hogan wants to chew you out.

I've never cared much for lingo. As I said, I have a BA in English from the University of Colorado at Denver. I killed time in my youth reading classic literature before deciding to stick with cab driving instead of cranking out English majors like sausages, which is the only thing a BA in English is good for: making little BAs. Some of my friends went on to get their Ph.D.'s so they could teach English and they haven't been heard from since.

But lingo is my life now. There's no getting away from it in this era of 24/7. When I worked at Dyna-Plex, the other white-collars spent their days hanging around the water cooler saying things like "reinvent the wheel," or "more bang for your buck," or "work smarter, not harder." A man can stand only so much self-motivation before he starts driving a taxi. He starts listening for bells. If he's lucky, he's one block away when the radio barks "L-5 Hilton!" But I heard only standard audio traffic that morning: pickup at King Soopers, Aurora Mall, CU Blood Bank. I finally gave up pretending to work hard. I decided to head downtown and check out the length of the cab lines at the hotels.

After I got parked in front of the Brown Palace, I took ten seconds to primp. I looked at my shag in the rear-view mirror, pulled a fast comb-job, checked my teeth for moths, and sat back. I always primp before going into action. The executives at Rocky constantly remind us cabbies that good hygiene translates into good tips. They won't get an argument out of me.

But one look at my hair reminded me of something I would rather have forgotten: Gino's. I decided that if any of my trips took me down east Colfax I would take a look at Gino's as I passed by, just to see where my nervous bailout from the day before worked. I was kidding myself, of course. I knew I would end up walking though his door one of these days. I had spent a restless night dreaming about my Maw back in Wichita. "It's free, fer the luvva Christ!" she kept saying. She's second generation Irish-Catholic. Nuff said.

There were three taxis parked ahead of me at the Brown. I sipped my steaming coffee and thought about turning on the AM radio and catching the morning news. But it was too early for news. It's always too early for news.

Half an hour later I was first in line at the Brown, the caffeine was giving my system a nice massage, and I was primed for my first customer. Then the back door of my cab opened and a pedestrian got in.

I glanced around expecting the Gino man, but it was a street person, late-twenties, unwashed, unemployed, and looking for trouble.

"Take me to Colfax and Broadway," he said.

I eased around and looked him in the eye. I flipped my Rolodex and stopped at D for disgust. "Colfax and Broadway is a couple blocks over," I said. "You can walk there."

He grinned and said. "Okay, take me up to Capitol Hill."

I sighed, dropped my red flag, and said a small prayer to the god of shuffles. I drove him over to Colfax and carted him up the hill past the Capitol building with its golden dome sparkling in the morning light. I let this farce continue for another two blocks, then I said, "Where do you want me to let you out?"

"I don't have any money," he said.

I glanced back at him.

"What?"

"I don't have any money."

I shut off the meter, pulled the cab over to the curb, and parked. I turned all the way around in my seat so I would have access to both of my hands. "Get out," I said.

The man didn't seem to be drunk, no telltale odor of alcohol, but maybe he was a pill-head. He grinned again and said, "What do you mean?"

"I mean get out of my taxi."

"Just like that?" he said, as though he had been expecting a more complex dialogue, a more satisfying resolution, or perhaps a slap in the chops.

"Just like that," I said.

He seemed disappointed. He shrugged and opened the door, climbed out and closed it. I drove back toward the Brown Palace reciting the Cab Driver's Prayer—to wit: "It doesn't matter, it doesn't matter, it doesn't matter."

Whenever a pedestrian gives me grief, I have learned to simply drive away and console myself with the knowledge that his presence on earth is his own punishment. But the scene rang a bell in my memory. It had the feel of an O. Henry tale—"The Cop and the Anthem." The only thing I really like about O. Henry is the fact that he spent three years in prison for embezzlement. That practically justifies his literary career, and believe me, it needs it.

CHAPTER 4

As I approached the Brown I gave up all hope. There were six cabs parked in the line. I was playing a losing game. I kept driving. I decided to head to the DOT clinic and take my physical. I had considered waiting until Friday to get naked, but my plans are a lot like algebra class. I failed algebra.

I circled up past the Capitol again and kept my eye out for the troublemaker. You wonder about the lives of people like that, wandering around broke, grinning like goons, useless and hopeless. It reminded me of college.

I did two years at Kansas Agricultural University before I left Wichita with my heart packed in a suitcase. KAU was the home of the Bovines. The Bovines was the name of the football team—I think. But I try not to think about the reason I left the Jayhawker State. I try not to think about Mary Margaret Flaherty.

I stayed on Colfax Avenue all the way past Monaco Parkway. I started looking for the barbershop. I pulled the business card out of my shirt pocket. I had taken it from the corkboard before leaving my apartment that morning. I intended to let the card hang for awhile, like that free pass to Putt-Putt, but as I was walking out the door I heard the voice of my Maw saying, "Yeh forgot something, boy-o."

I peered at the address. I had a mile to go. I tucked the card back into my shirt pocket and gazed upon the wonders of east Colfax, the gateway to Aurora. I passed the neighborhood where the blind man lived. His house was two blocks north.

All right. Here's my blind man story:

Thirteen years ago I picked up a blind man at Union Station. He had just come in from Oakland, California, on the Zephyr. He wanted to go to east Denver. When we got there, the meter came to $16.40. He handed me a twenty and told me to keep a dollar for myself. And because I was new at driving, and because I had failed arithmetic in grade school, and because my hearing is dyslexic, I reached into my shirt pocket, pulled out a dollar bill, and handed it to him. He climbed out and made his way up the sidewalk, and I drove off. Ten minutes later I got a call from the dispatcher (code phrase "L-2") telling me to bring my cab in to the motor. Hogan wanted to talk to me. When I arrived at the motor, Hogan told me that an angry blind man had called and said I short-changed him and made off with nineteen dollars instead of seventeen-forty. I felt like I was back in grade school being chastised by a nun. I had to explain myself. Have you ever tried to explain yourself? If not, I don't recommend it. But because Hogan is a smart man who can read a cabbie like an X-ray, he believed me. I had to drive back to the fare's house and give him the correct change. Brother, you don't know the meaning of the word "humiliation" until you've apologized to a blind man who couldn't read an X-ray on his best day and doesn't believe a word you say.

End of story.

The sign said "Gino's Barbershop." I made a circle of the block and pulled up in front. I sat there thinking it might be a good idea to get a free haircut before I took my DOT physical. I didn't know how much hair weighed, but I had a feeling the DOT doctor wasn't going to be impressed by the collection of cellulite that I store under my belt. I had purchased it at Sweeney's Tavern.

Sweeney had recently hired a graduate of a bartending school, a kid named Harold. Harold is a runner, and he always manages to work that unfortunate fact into his conversations. He tells me I ought to join him at the YMCA for a mile run. But he's young.

There's still plenty of time to make him understand that nobody ever wants to do anything.

I climbed out of my cab and walked up to the shop and peered through the plateglass window. Someone was moving around inside. Someone in a white smock.

Bells rang over the door as I walked in. I inhaled old wood and Butch Wax. It smelled good. A white-haired man was pushing a broom, making a pile of used hair on the floor. Three chairs, no waiting. He turned and gazed at me querulously. Then his eyes were drawn to my shag.

"May I help you?" he said. He had an Italian accent.

I began to feel foolish. I saw myself through his eyes, a man in his mid-forties with a head like a hippie who obviously cut his own shag. What was this joker doing in my barbershop?

I quickly pulled out the business card and held it up for him to see. "I'm looking for Gino," I said.

"I'm Gino," he replied.

"Well, I guess I'm not looking for Gino," I said, going for a gag. A dark shadow crossed his face. "What I mean is," I continued quickly, "one of your employees gave me this card and told me to drop by sometime."

He approached me with the broom held in both hands like a rifle at port arms. He raised his chin and squinted at the card.

"That belongs to Tony," he said.

"Then I'm looking for Tony," I said. Before I could explain, his eyes got hard and he raised the broom a few inches.

"Whaddya want with Tony?"

"Like I said, he gave me this card yesterday and told me he would give me a free haircut."

He squinted at me. "Tony isn't here. Where'd you meet Tony?" The atmosphere in the room was getting heavy. I pointed through the plateglass window. "That's my taxicab outside. I picked up Tony yesterday at the Hilton Hotel downtown. He gave me his card and said to drop by."

The man raised his chin a little higher and looked through the window. "Where did you take Tony?" he said.

"I didn't take him anywhere. He changed his mind and got out."

"Got out? What do you mean he got out?"

"I mean he got in, decided not to go anywhere, and got out of my taxi."

"What was Tony doing at the Hilton Hotel?"

I slipped the card into my pocket and stepped back. "Maybe I'll drop by sometime later," I said. "Could you tell him the cab driver came by?"

"Wait a minute," he said. "What time was Tony at the Hilton Hotel?"

I thought fast. "I don't remember exactly. I get a lot of customers. It was sometime yesterday."

"And you say he got into your cab, changed his mind, and got back out?"

"Yes, sir."

"Why would Tony do that?"

"I don't know, sir. I'm just a taxi driver."

He gave me a long slow study from my shag to my tennis shoes. "What's your name?" he said.

Suddenly I wished I had stayed in Wichita. "Murph," I replied.

"Murph," he said soundlessly.

I started walking backward. "So anyway, could you please tell Tony that I was here? I'll drop by some other day," in your dreams.

I opened the door and backed out, hurried around my cab and got in. As I started the engine I looked at the front door. The old man was staring at me through the glass. He raised one hand, took hold of the OPEN sign, and flipped it to CLOSED.

I got the hell out of there.

CHAPTER 5

We've all gone through physicals. The first time I coughed for a saw-bones I was in the Boy Scouts. Wichita, Kansas. Summer camp. I was ten. Before we scouts were allowed to spend a week at Camp Wa-Ni-Ta-Ka we had to prove we didn't have hernias. One look at me should have convinced the doc. I was as skinny as Olive Oyl and hadn't touched a base-ball since first grade. My idea of summer activities was to turn on the TV while my evil brother Gavin headed for Little League.

But I passed the Boy Scout physical and spent a week at Camp Wa-Ni-Ta-Ka. It was hell. Tents, outhouses, no TV. I don't like to think about it. I did manage to steal ten dollars from an Eagle Scout, but that's a long story. Let's drop it.

Prior to driving over to DOT, I stopped at a 7-11 on Quebec Street. Mickey was behind the cash register. Mickey is a former cabbie who quit the business after he got married. "I need a steady paycheck, Murph," he told me the day I walked in and saw him slinging Slurpees. But I under-stood. Hacking is a bachelor's game. I know a lot of married cabbies, but they own their cabs and work five days a week like real people. They live in a completely different world from mine. I drive whenever I feel like it. For instance, if the Broncos are playing Monday Night Football, the streets of Denver will not be graced with my presence.

"Time for my physical again, Mickey," I said with a sigh.

Mickey nodded and poured three paper cups full of water. I always drink three cups before going in for my urine test. I like to think of it as a "plan," but Mickey refers to it as my "annual desperation move." This might be a problem of semantics. My plans never work but my desperation moves are surprisingly effective. I've seen long-haul truck drivers shyly wandering up and down the halls of DOT waiting for the coffee provided by the nurse to kick in. "Anything yet?" the nurse will say in front of the entire waiting room. Truckers who look big enough to juggle strippers will shake their heads no and hurry away in shame.

"What looks good in the lottery, Mick?" I said, gazing at the scratch games tucked safely under the glass of the countertop.

Mickey shook his head and grinned. "Don't be a sucker, Murph."

I ignored his warning. He was married. He lived on another plane of existence altogether. Some people call it "adulthood."

"How's the Magic Carpet Cash doing?" I said, pointing at a scratch ticket covered with little green flying carpets.

Mickey sighed and shook his head no.

"How about Eureka Motherlode!?" I said, pointing at a ticket with a little bearded sourdough doing an Irish jig.

"Give it up, Murph," Mickey said as I drained the last cup of water. "The odds of winning a million bucks are zero."

I set my empty on the counter and smiled. "The odds of everything are zero, Mick. Just hand me five Pot-o'-Gold tickets and I'm outta here."

I won't bore you with the results.

I arrived at the DOT clinic a little before ten A.M. I took a number from the dispensing machine at the front counter where the clerks were processing the twenty-five dollar fee and sat down to wait. I was an old hand at waiting. I had learned to wait well in the army, and had taken the lesson home with me. Cheap lessons never stick in your mind the way the expensive ones do.

I pulled a paperback out of my jacket pocket but barely got a page read before my name was called. A nurse led me to the rear of the building. First order of business: urine. She handed me a small plastic cup, pointed at a door, and told me to give her a specimen.

The toilet was right off the hallway. A quick shot and the cup was full, then I had to spend two minutes emptying the rest of Mickey's water. Overkill trumps planning any day.

The nurse led me to the eye test. I wasn't worried. I had enjoyed 20/20 vision from day one. I squinted, flexed my eyeballs, and made uneducated guesses at the letters or else numbers on the test card, I couldn't tell which. I stood up from the machine, and the nurse gave me a bright smile.

"You need glasses," she said.

My ego took a direct hit. Me—a four-eyed freak. It was at that moment that I realized I was no longer a kid. I had gone through the army without glasses, had gone through college, had gone through life in a blur, but maybe things were clearer when I was young. This made me want to go home and forget the whole scene, but I couldn't. I needed glasses because my taxi was my meal ticket, my last hope—the only alternative was alleys and wine and a slow and merciless death putting the cap on a slow and merciless life.

The nurse led me down the hallway to a small room where she handed me a paper dress. It was time to get naked in front of a man.

Let's jump ahead ten minutes and try not to think about it.

I finished putting my clothes back on and walked down the hallway to the lobby where the nurse explained what had to be done.

"As soon as you get your glasses, come back and we'll give you the eye test again, and then you'll be certified."

I thanked her, left the building, got into my cab, and leaned back against the seat. I sighed. Nothing can be easy. Everything has to be hard. I figured I might as well drive back to Rocky and turn in my cab. Wednesday was a wash. I had to find an optometrist fast. Glasses. Who invented glasses? But I knew who. The Chinese.

I drove back toward Rocky thinking about hair and eyeballs. Maybe I would return to Gino's when Tony was there and get that freebie. New wig, four eyes, a complete makeover. These are the kinds of thoughts an asphalt warrior has when death starts closing in.

I parked at the motor and went inside, passed through the on-call room and knocked on the door to Sheila's office. Sheila is a black woman who has been working at the motor since before my time. She's the head secretary. She takes care of the important paperwork, the DOT reports, applications for jobs, the map test you have to pass before they send you down to the City and County Building to repeat the map test for the mayor. She was surprised to see me back so early. I told her about the glasses.

Sheila dresses to the nines every day. Coiffed hair, gold earrings, painted eyelashes, ruby lipstick, gold-chain necklaces, flowery dresses, and I've never seen her wearing the same pair of shoes twice. She's one class act. But her most striking accoutrement is her big red girl-glasses. The frames are perfect circles, three inches in diameter.

"Are you nearsighted or farsighted?" Sheila said. I had no idea.

"Try these on." She removed her glasses and handed them to me.

I slipped them on, and the world snapped into focus. The far wall wasn't just a brown wall; it had a wooden texture. When I looked at Sheila I could see individual strands of her hair, and molded details of her earrings. It was like I had burst through the surface of a murky pond into the transparent miracle of air.

"Can you see better?" she said. I nodded.

"I'll call the clinic and tell them you're coming back," Sheila said. She was dialing the phone before I could voice an objection.

She hung up the receiver. "They're expecting you."

I walked outside and got into 127 and sat for a moment trying the glasses on. I could see a stop sign at the end of the block, which became a blur when I raised the glasses and looked with my naked eyes. Some things in life are not a crock, and a pair of glasses is one of them.

All the way to the clinic I kept raising and lowering the glasses, marveling at how soft shapes in the distance clicked into approaching cars, telephone poles, pedestrians. I looked at myself in the rear-view mirror. Who was I kidding? Nobody at the clinic would believe a cab driver owned big red girl-glasses. I had to think fast. I needed a plan. I stopped playing with my eyeballs and got down to business.

When I arrived at the clinic I took off the specs and tucked them into my shirt pocket. I went inside and gave my name, said the cab company had sent me back over. The clerk nodded, told me to have a seat.

I sat down on a chair in the lobby and pulled out my paperback.

"Did you get new glasses?"

I lowered the book. The nurse was standing directly in front of me. Bright eyed. Big smile. I nodded and touched my breast pocket where the specs were hidden.

"Put 'em on!" she sang out. "Let's see 'em!" Fer the luvva Christ.

I glanced around the lobby. No place to run. I reached into my pocket, pulled out the big red girl-glasses and put them on.

The smile faded from her face. She stared at me for a few hours, then she said, "They're nice," and walked away. I knew I was nailed. I would be pounding the pavement the next morning looking for a new job, preferably one that didn't require eyesight.

I took off the glasses and stuck them into my shirt pocket. A different nurse approached and asked me to accompany her to the eye station. I got up and slouched over to the machine. I didn't put the glasses on until I was leaning down to look through the binoculars. Before I stood erect I quickly removed them and slipped them into my pocket. The essence of my "plan" consisted of sneakiness.

I did pass the eye test, and was given my medical papers to take back to Rocky Cab. Don't ask me how it happened, but I didn't get nailed. You can carve that on my tombstone.

CHAPTER 6

When I got back to my crow's nest I wasn't as tired as I usually am after work, especially since I hadn't worked. Sometimes I work six-hour shifts, sometimes I work twelve-hour shifts. It depends on different factors, sometimes money, sometimes disgust. If I've earned a lot of either, I quit for the day. I occasionally squeeze fourteen hours out of a shift on a slow night, but keep that under your hat. It's illegal, like almost everything else I wish I had the guts to do.

I tossed my plastic briefcase onto the kitchen counter, reached into my shirt pocket, plucked out the Gino card and dropped it next to the briefcase. I didn't want to think about haircuts and eyeballs anymore. I decided to turn my brain off for the night. I decided to write.

I'm an unpublished writer. All cab drivers are unpublished writers. It's the rule of the road. A lot of cab drivers write because they have degrees in English. I'm Exhibit A. But some drivers don't have any excuse for writing. They just do it.

I opened the fridge, took out a brew, popped the top, took a sip, and sat down at the kitchen table. I didn't know whether to work on the novels or the screenplays. Yeah. You heard me right. Plurals. I had so many unpublished manuscripts lying around my apartment I felt like a literary agent.

I own a steamer trunk filled with old manuscripts that I've been hauling around ever since I left Wichita. It contains every short story, novel, and screenplay I've ever written. I was an undergraduate when I made my first attempt at a novel. It rests in its place of honor at the bottom of my steamer trunk. It's called *The Planet of the Suffering Fools*. It's about a planet where these mammal-like humanoids have lives that are miserable and meaningless, but no matter how much they suffer they do everything they can to stay alive because—"every breath they take seems like a gift from Santa Claus." The main character is a twenty-year-old who can't make any sense out of his existence. I never finished it. I couldn't make any sense out of the plot. I'm proud to say, however, that my steamer trunk does not now contain, nor has it ever contained, a poem.

After college, the stacks of manuscripts became so unwieldy that I decided I needed some way to file and sort them, but in the end I bought the steamer trunk at a flea market and just tossed them in there. When they began to overflow the trunk, I started building my bookshelves. I use only the thickest unpublished manuscripts in place of bricks. If I could figure out a way to replace the wood-plank shelving with unfinished manuscripts I would do it, but I don't want to get bogged down in that aspect of creative writing.

That's one of the many lessons about writing that I have learned over the years. A writer can become obsessed with the peripheral rituals of writing—such as sharpening pencils or visiting the Grand Canyon—when he should be focused on the most important part of writing, which is leafing through *Writers Market* and making lists of agents who don't charge reading fees. I've written a lot of novels over the years. My greatest ambition in life is to be destroyed by fame.

But the notion of going to all the trouble of digging and sorting through my steamer trunk looking for something to work on ultimately killed my desire to write. It doesn't take much to cause me to give up on the little dream. Every cab driver dreams the little dream of finding free time to sit down in front of a typewriter. But when he finds it, somehow the little dream never comes true. By "he" I mean "I."

For the English professors out there who are starting to squirm, by "finds" I mean "find."

Breathe deeply and say "Om," okay?

I went into the living room and hit the TV remote. But I couldn't concentrate on the shows. I kept squinting at the glass face of the cathode-ray tube, bringing it in and out of focus. A dark thought hit me. What if I bought a pair of glasses and discovered that I didn't really enjoy what I thought I had been enjoying ever since me Mither sweet-talked me ol' Dad into buying a Motorola when I was a lad? What if the glasses brought everything into focus and killed my last hope?

I shut off the TV, drained the beer, and got up. Reality was starting to crowd me. Who the hell invented "reality"? I'd had my fill of it for one day. I turned off the lights, went into the bedroom, kicked off my Keds, and collapsed into bed.

I chose not to track down an optometrist on Thursday morning. Instead I opted for denial. I had survived all these years without wearing corrective lenses, so one more cab shift shouldn't tempt the hand of Fate. Two shifts even. But I knew that within a week's time Sheila would be tapping those classy toes of hers and reminding me that Rocky Cab had gone one hundred and ninety-six days without an accident on the books.

Rollo handed me my key and trip-sheet without saying a word. Apparently he didn't know the upshot of my physical. Believe me, he's the kind of guy who would put a hold on my key until I crossed all the tees and dotted my eyes with safety lenses. I knew I had Sheila to thank for this. She was the hard case I would have to deal with if I didn't grow up soon.

I drove downtown with a cup of 7-11 joe in one hand and a Twinkie tucked into my briefcase. I parked third in line at the Brown Palace. The morning streets were quiet. Rush hour hadn't begun yet. Rush hours are interesting. Cars appear like random hailstones here and there—and then comes the deluge, a horn-honking hurricane that lasts an hour. Then the ebb tide. It's like everybody in Denver is programmed to go nuts at seven in the morning. I guess they are. Even though I drive during the rush hour, I never feel like a member of the masses hurrying off to their jobs. I feel more like ramrod Rowdy Yates riding herd on longhorns. I highly recommend denial to anyone who works for a living.

I made a few short runs around town, down to Cherry Creek Shopping Center, up to Capitol Hill, no airport trips, no big scores. And then, at eleven o'clock, just as I was driving toward the Hilton to check out the length of the taxi line, I saw Tony the barber. He was wearing the same black overcoat he had been wearing on Monday. He was walking slowly along the line of cabs, bending down and looking inside each one. It gave me a funny feeling.

I averted my face and cruised on past the Hilton. What was Tony doing checking out every cab in line? Was he looking for one driver in particular? Was he looking for me?

That was the funny feeling.

I drove toward Union Station as I mulled this over. Maybe Tony was just checking out haircuts. Believe me, Rocky had plenty of cabbies who needed a card from Tony.

But something told me that Tony wasn't trying to network. I cruised past Union Station just to see if any trains had come in. The Rocky Cab dispatcher makes an announcement if Union Station needs taxis. But the station was dead. I drove up past the Oxford Hotel and thought about parking out front and listening for radio calls, but I kept thinking about Tony. What was he—as Gino had asked me—doing at the Hilton Hotel? I decided to drive back and take another look.

I swung over to 15th Street and headed back up toward midtown so I could come at the Hilton from a distance. I turned onto Welton Street and slowed, and looked, and saw him. It was Tony all right. Only now he was just standing in front of the Hilton looking slowly back and forth.

The light at 17th turned red. I stopped at the corner. I stared at Tony. I was trying to decide whether or not to drive away or call my own bluff and pull in at the rear of the line, get out and tell him I had dropped by and spoken to Gino. But the decision was made for me. Tony turned and stepped into the Hilton. I waited for the light to turn green, then I made a right and drove over to Broadway. I decided to avoid the Hilton Hotel for the rest of my life.

To tell you the truth, I never much like it when I get the same customer in my cab twice. The reason for this is fairly complex, but part of it has to do with the fear that I might run into someone who thinks that two meetings with me constitute a lifelong friendship. And part has to do with my general desire for anonymity. On top of that, being a fraud takes a lot of energy out of me. If a group of young executives gets into my cab, I become a literate, well-informed college grad picking up some money part-time driving a taxi. If an old lady gets into my cab, I become her favorite grandson. I won't even try to describe my Jekyll-and-Hyde persona when a hardcore politico hops in. Trying to figure out whether you've got a Republican or a Democrat in your backseat is a high-wire act that can test the mettle of the most experienced cabbie. So the strain of becoming twenty different people a day is bad enough without trying to keep track of who I was last week. I'm sure the abnormal psychology textbooks have a technical term for this phenomenon, but I just refer to it as "being me."

I turned on the two-way radio and listened to the calls. The dispatcher yelled at a few newbies. Dispatchers are sort of like drill sergeants in the army. They take no guff from the drivers. Their bark is indistinguishable from their bite. They'll pull a surly cabbie off the street without hesitation and send him to the commanding officer (Hogan). Cabbies are always grumbling among themselves about what bastards the dispatchers are, but after you've been driving as long as I have, you laugh whenever you hear a dispatcher screaming his head off at some novice who forgot to write down the address he was supposed to go to. Dispatching calls over the radio is a hard job, fast-paced and unforgiving, but those men and women who work the transmitter mold new recruits into asphalt warriors. They can either make you or break you, and if they break you, it's time to start looking for a real job.

"UCD," the dispatcher said. I picked up my mike before any other driver snatched the call away from me. "One twenty-seven," I said.

A student at the University of Colorado at Denver needed a ride. He was waiting for me down at the Tivoli, a nineteenth-century brewery that had been remodeled into a shopping complex near the UCD campus. I swung over to west Colfax and headed toward my alma mater.

CHAPTER 7

The kid was standing near a phone booth in the Tivoli parking lot. He had a book bag swung over one shoulder. His hair was short. Mine was long. The Generation Gap had pulled a one-eighty during the past twenty years. He climbed into the backseat and sat with his book bag on his lap.

"I'm going to North Denver," he said. He gave me an address near the old Elitch's Amusement Park site. I clenched my teeth and grinned. This was a sweet score, fifteen bucks maybe.

"Do you want to go I-25 or up Federal Boulevard?" I said.

"It doesn't matter," he said. He seemed morose, but then he was a college student. Show me a college student who isn't morose and I'll show you a kid who hasn't read Dostoevsky.

I got onto the highway and headed north, following the bed of the Platte River toward the I-70 interchange.

"How long have you been a student?" I said.

He gave up a small sigh. "Almost three years. I'm a junior." He didn't elaborate.

I ran his tone of voice and body language through the Univac that all cabbies possess, a mental computer similar to my Rolodex. It spat out a punch card, which indicated the kid didn't want to talk. But we had a long way to go before I got off the highway.

"What's your major?" I said.

"English."

I froze.

This was a delicate situation. I had been thinking about telling him that I was a graduate of UCD with a BA in English, but this might forge one of those bonds that I deliberately avoid. Put two English majors to-gether in a confined space, and the next thing you know you're discussing Sir Gawain.

"Do you plan to teach after you graduate?" I said, attempting to bring closure to this conversation as painlessly as possible.

The kid gave up another sigh. "I'm not sure I'm going to graduate."

"Why is that?" I said, trying not to sound too nosy, which I am good at. I said it fast, fiddling with the radio and adjusting my side mirror, giving all the indications that his future meant less to me than the life of a gnat.

"I'm thinking of dropping out," he replied, his voice so mournful and despondent that my heart soared like an eagle. This was a kid who needed my help.

"Why drop out?" I said.

"I don't see any point to it all."

I raised my chin so I could look at him in the mirror as we rolled along. "I graduated from UCD fifteen years ago with a degree in English," I said.

"Really?" he said, as he gazed around the backseat—at the floor, at the roof, at the back of my head. I knew what he was thinking: what's an Eng-lish grad doing in a hack?

"In fact, it took me seven years to get my degree," I said. "I was in no hurry to go to work. Most of my friends got their degrees in four years, and half of them are teaching English. The other half are in-house writers for corporate magazines."

"Do you drive a cab full time?"

"In a sense," I replied. "This is what I do for a living, but I can't say I drive full time. I pretty much drive whenever I want. After graduating from UCD I decided to find a job that was as much like college as possible, minus the homework. Cab driving filled the bill."

His expression changed from mournfulness to wonder.

"I take it you haven't decided whether or not to drop out," I said.

"My mother is paying for my education. That's where I'm headed now, to see my mother. She really wants me to get my degree. So does my girlfriend."

Ouch. Girlfriend.

This was an added factor that multiplied the problem in a geometrical progression of potential grief. "Do you plan to get married after you graduate?" I said.

This was a highly personal question, but I had found that fares didn't seem to mind talking about their private lives with a cabbie, maybe because the relationship between a cabbie and a fare is traditionally brief and meaningless, like a lot of marriages. "Yeah. We were going to wait a couple years, but if I drop out now, she'll want me to get a job and marry her right away."

This kid was way ahead of me. I liked that. But he didn't know how to wrestle with a problem that could make him or break him on the long road to the last supper.

"I dropped out once," I said. "It was at the end of my sophomore year at Kansas Agricultural University. Biggest mistake I ever made. I had to get a job. My Maw was willing to support me as long as I was going for an English degree. But brother, let me tell you, as soon as I came home and announced that I was quitting school, my Maw handed me the classified ads and started tapping the Help Wanted columns. When that didn't sink in, she flipped the page over to the For Rent section and told me I had twenty-four hours to vacate the premises."

I glanced around at his expression. I couldn't tell if it was fear or laughter. That was nothing new to me. I see that expression in my bathroom mirror every morning.

"But I was kind of a rebel back then," I continued. "I called her bluff. I took what was left of my GI Bill money, split town, and started eating hamburgers for breakfast."

"Why did you drop out of school?" he said.

"I was in love. Her name was Mary Margaret Flaherty. I wanted to marry her. So as you can see, our situations are slightly reversed. But she wasn't about to marry a dropout. I left Wichita and moved to Denver, trying to forget my past. I've spent approximately—let's see if I can remember now—twenty years trying to forget my past. No luck so far."

"How did you get started in cab driving?" he said.

"A college buddy of mine turned me on to it," I said. "That's how most cabbies get started. It seemed like an easy way to pick up some extra money during school. At first I just sort of dabbled in it. Next thing I knew I was doing it every weekend. By the time I graduated I was a mainliner, hooked for life. It beats the hell out of working, but I have to be honest with you, I'd rather be in college. I miss sleeping till noon seven days a week. I'm lucky now if I can take Tuesday and Thursday off. But when the rent comes due I have to drive five days in a row. That's why I'm on the road today. Next week I'm taking my monthly spring break." I pulled into the right lane and slowed for the interchange, which I call Agatha Christie Boulevard. The city of Denver calls it the Mousetrap. Ever since it was constructed in the 1950s its been the site of more bottlenecks than Coca-Cola. The city keeps remodeling it. I'm sure they'll get it right one of these days. I swung around the loop and drove up onto I-70 headed west. We were halfway there.

"Did you ever plan to teach English?" he said.

"Nah. Me and grammar rules ain't compatible. It gives me the willies to think of me molding young minds. That's what my old college chums do with their Ph.D.'s though. They write letters every so often from Ivy League schools back East and tell me funny stories about the vicissitudes of inter-departmental politics. You wouldn't believe how cutthroat a professor of medieval literature can get when he comes up for tenure. There's blood on the blackboards."

I glanced at the kid in the mirror. Normally I don't hand out advice unless fares explicitly ask for it, but this was an emergency.

"If I were you I'd stay in school," I said. "Look at it this way. You're guaranteed to remain single for another year. You don't have to crawl out of bed at dawn every morning and go to a job you hate. And you'll have plenty of time to figure your next move. Who knows? You might decide to go to grad school and stay single for as long as it takes to finish your Ph.D. thesis. Hell, I've got a buddy who drives a cab in Portland and he's been working on his thesis for ten years."

The kid looked like he had just awakened from a hypnotic trance. I could practically hear the wheels turning inside his head. Then I reeled him in.

"And there's always room for one more at Rocky Cab."

The meter came to just under fifteen dollars. He began digging into his billfold. I parked in front of his house. He handed me a twenty.

"Keep the change," he said.

"Gosh, thanks," I said obsequiously. "And good luck."

He climbed out and walked up to his mother's house with a swing in his step.

That was the easiest double sawbuck I ever made. Twenty is one number I get along with just fine.

CHAPTER 8

I pulled around the corner and parked my cab. I wanted to fill out my trip-sheet and stow my cash. Just taking care of business. As I tucked the twenty into my billfold, I hoped I hadn't ruined the kid's life. I often hope that.

Just so you know, I didn't start driving cabs in college. That came after I dropped out of Dyna-Plex. Writers often incorporate the experiences of real-life acquaintances into their stories. So do liars.

As far as Mary Margaret Flaherty not wanting to marry a dropout ... well, that part was true. But I think it had more to do with her not wanting to marry an unpublished novelist. "How long do you think it will take you to start making money at it?" she asked me one night. We were courting at the time. I think the thing that tipped the scales against me was when I told her I didn't write for money. Yeah. I'm pretty sure that's what made her pink cheeks go pale. I tried to explain that money either comes or it doesn't, but that a real writer is concerned only with his art. I read that in a how-to book. Then she asked me how I intended to earn money so that we could afford to buy a house after we got married. That made my own cheeks go pale. But I don't want to go into the details of The Big Breakup. I'm somewhat of a fan of minimalism in literature, so the verb "nosedive" ought to sum it up.

As an aside, did you know that the word "verb" is a noun? Don't ask me to explain it. Ask Franz Kafka.

I drove along 38th Avenue back toward downtown Denver and tried not to look at the demolished Elitch's site as I headed east. Twenty years ago, after I first came to Denver, Elitch's Amusement Park was where I went at night when I was broke, lonely, and looking for cotton candy. The Elitch

Theater is still standing. I once saw Mickey Rooney come out of the theater. He was starring in a play. After the show ended, he came striding out a side door with a big grin on his face and headed for the parking lot. I froze. Mickey—star of silent movies, talkies, and frequent guest on Steve Allen. I didn't even think to ask for his autograph. He was gone in an instant. Mickey Rooney fascinates me.

I drove as far as Fox Street, then cut across the viaduct past the Rockies baseball stadium and found myself cruising along Wynkoop Street in the direction of Union Station. Full circle. Standard operating procedure in a taxi.

When I drove up past the Oxford Hotel I started thinking about Tony the barber. Why was he at the Hilton again? When Gino had asked me what Tony was doing there, I got the funny feeling that Tony wasn't supposed to be anywhere near the place on Monday. I couldn't block out the image of Tony looking into taxis like he was looking for a familiar face. My face. I hate it when people look for me. Sergeants were always looking for me in the army. Sergeants with mops. But back then I figured all I had to do was hide out for two years and I was home free. It worked.

I decided to park at the Fairmont Hotel cabstand. I pulled up fourth in line. I shut everything off— my engine, my two-way radio, my AM radio, and my paperback. I sat there watching the front door. The doorman at the Fairmont is named Jules. He was doing his doorman dance, directing porters, greeting guests, opening cab doors, and discreetly pocketing tips.

Doormen and cabbies have a lot in common, except doormen wear white gloves and classy long coats with brass buttons. You never really get chummy with hotel doormen, but palace guards and asphalt warriors respect each other and do each other favors as the occasion arises. There is honor among men who thrive on tips.

I get along well with both Jules and Francois. On a number of occasions I have escorted slobbering drunks out of the Hilton bar at the request of Francois and driven them home. In return, he sometimes passes The Word along if a group of guests are planning a trip to Vail or Aspen. I took a group of skiers to Vail one winter day many years ago and it turned into The Trip From Hell. I don't want to talk about it.

An elderly couple came out of the hotel. I cruised up to the door. Jules leaned down to my window and said, somewhat apologetically, that they wanted to go to Larimer Square. Larimer Square is only a few blocks away. Normally this would have annoyed me, but I just grinned at Jules and nodded. This was one of those favors I mentioned, but subtle if you know what I mean. No whining. Doormen hate it when cabbies whine, but who doesn't? The next time I showed up, Jules might deal me a guest headed for the Grand Canyon.

"We're from Chicago," the woman said brightly after she and her husband got settled in the backseat.

"The home of the hawk," I said as I started the meter. "The Windy City." They seemed to like that. As I pulled out they asked if I would drive them around downtown before dropping them off—they had never been to Denver before.

I hauled them over to the Capitol building so they could look at the massive dome of authentic gold leaf. The woman pulled a Nikon out of her purse and snapped a picture. "For my grandchildren." I gave them a quick narrative of Denver history, making up the parts I was unsure of. I had gotten a B in my history class at UCD, but that college course about Denver's past had come in handier than any Latin class I had ever taken in high school.

Next, I ran them over to admire the Brown Palace. The woman snapped another picture. A lot of tourists seem to think the Brown Palace was named after The Unsinkable Molly Brown, but it's just a brownstone building that was erected by Horace Tabor, a silver baron who died broke. It's a long story. Let's move on.

I circled the block, pointing out the Ship Tavern at one corner of the building, a watering hole where famous authors are sometimes feted during book tours. And there stood Tony. He was bending down and peering into taxis. I got rattled. I damn near stopped my cab and told the couple that the Brown Palace was a part of Larimer Square. They wouldn't have known. They were from Chicago.

But I kept driving. I had to dump those two rubes fast. I told them we had better get over to Larimer Square quick so they wouldn't miss the mock gunfight between Wyatt Earp and Soapy Smith, which wasn't true. I don't know if you know anything about Denver, but any gunfights that take place in this town aren't mock. Larimer Square is just a collection of trendy restaurants and boutiques, like California.

They thanked me for my educational tour and gave me ten bucks on a four-dollar meter. I saluted and got the hell out of there. I headed back toward Broadway. I was determined to catch up with Tony.

I circled the Brown Palace and came up on the rear of the cab line but I didn't see Tony anywhere. This was worse than phone tag. I parked and got out and walked up to the next cab in line, a Rocky Cab. Big Al was sitting in the driver's seat checking out the names of dogs running at the kennel club.

"What's popping?" I said, leaning into his window.

"Ricky Rocket in the sixth," he replied, tapping the tip-sheet in his hand. "Ten bucks on the nose."

"I had a personal that got away from me," I lied. "I was supposed to meet him here but I got tied up. Did you happen to see a guy in a long black overcoat? He might have been looking for me."

A "personal" is a fare you pick up on a regular basis, such as from his home every morning. You make a mutual agreement ahead of time. I steer clear of personals. They can get in the way of airport runs.

Big Al lowered the tip-sheet and squinted at me. "Maybe."

"What do you mean, maybe?"

"There was a stranger here awhile ago asking questions."

"What kind of questions?"

"Questions about a driver who looked like you."

"Like me how?"

"Like a guy who cuts his own hair." I got embarrassed fast.

"Where did he go?" I said.

Big Al shrugged. "I been busy," he said, tapping the tip-sheet. I looked up and down the block and sighed. There were no pedestrians in sight, and no customers coming out of the Brown.

The street was dead.

"He'll find you," Big Al said.

"How do you know?"

"I told him to call Rocky Cab and ask for Murph."

It didn't surprise me that Big Al had taken so long to get to the damn point. He had been my trainer back when I was a newbie hack. He taught me everything I know about taxi driving, dog racing, and mind games.

Big Al drives Rocky Mountain Taxicab #61, the oldest as well as the last of the two-digit cabs in the fleet. He's been driving for twenty years. We get along well. At least, that's my take on it. I have never inquired as to his opinion of my take. I will say that he is somewhat of a cynic. When he isn't yanking my chain, he's rattling my gourd, but I endure it because, to be perfectly frank, I like to watch a master at work. I take prodigious notes.

His radio suddenly barked to life.

"One twenty-seven! One twenty-seven!"

"That's you, Tenderfoot," Big Al said. "Don't keep the man waiting."

I dashed back to my cab and grabbed the mike. The dispatcher told me I had a personal waiting at the corner of Broadway and Colfax. "The fare's name is Tony Bombalini."

CHAPTER 9

It took me less than a minute to get there. I saw Tony standing by a phone booth with his hands stuffed into his coat pockets and an anxious expression on his face. I see the same expression in my bathroom mirror after getting rejections slips from publishers and literary agents.

I pulled up to the curb and stopped. He opened the door and climbed in.

"I hear you've been looking for me," I said.

When he pulled his hands out of his pockets, I noticed they were no longer trembling. Now it was his eyes that were giving him away. In my line of work, and in my rear-view mirror, you see a lot of eyes. I know my eyes. He glanced at me a couple of times as he settled in, tugging at the hem of his coat as he shut the door. He hadn't spoken a word and already he was being evasive. I know all about evasion. I wrote the book.

"Yes ... I called your taxi company and specifically asked for you," he said in a voice so filled with equivocation that I felt like a mind reader. It made me feel good. "I have somewhere to go and I thought I would give you the trip in order to make up for the fact that I wasn't in my shop when you dropped by yesterday."

I put the cab into gear and pulled away from the curb, heading south on Broadway.

"That's right," I said, "I dropped by Gino's to see about that free haircut. You weren't around."

"I know, I'm sorry, I was out on some personal business. Perhaps we should have set an appointment ahead of time to meet. I really didn't think ..."

He paused.

So barbers took personals too, eh? I always figured old-fashioned bar-bers served only walk-ins, and surly teenagers with angry fathers.

"Didn't think what?" I said.

By now we were approaching the 11th Avenue Hotel and Tony still hadn't told me where he wanted to go. I hadn't even started the meter yet. I wanted to see if he would notice.

"Well it's just that ... I thought perhaps you might not ..."

"Show up at your shop?" I said.

"Well ..."

I decided to let him off the hook. "I gotcha, pal," I said. "I have a little confession to make to you. On Monday night I almost gave myself another sheep shearing. But then I found your card in my wallet and I said to my-self, 'Vanity, thy name is Murph.' Who was I to cut my own hair when I had a pro offering to do it for free? So I came around to your shop just to take you up on the offer. But you weren't in. I didn't bother to ask Gino if he would give me a free haircut. Hell, I got pedestrians coming up to my cab all the time and asking for free rides across town. To put it as kindly and gently as possible, I don't take them seriously."

This was true. Cab drivers and writers share one thing in common: a lot of people think they should be willing to work for free.

"I didn't think Gino was taking me very seriously either," I said.

"What do you mean?" he said.

"Well, I just mean that I do not look like the type of fellow who goes in for commercial haircuts. To tell you the truth, I got the feeling that Gino thought I was up to something, even after I showed him your business card. To stretch the truth even further, I got the feeling he thought I might have come in to rob the joint."

Tony let out a breathy chuckle and shook his head. "Gino is my uncle," he said. "He's a little high strung, but I'm sure he didn't think you were there to rob him. You were just a stranger. Most of our heads are old cus-tomers. He simply wasn't sure who you were."

"I hear you," I said. "No hard feelings."

By now we were coming up on Alameda Avenue, eighteen blocks from where we had started. The meter was off and I still hadn't asked Tony where he wanted to go. This told me everything I wanted to know, except why he was in my cab.

"Say ... will ya look at that?" I said. "I forgot to turn on my meter. Well, what the hell, turnabout is fair play. You give me a free haircut and I give you a free ride. As soon as you clip me, that'll make us square."

Tony's eyes went wide as he glanced at the meter. "My goodness," he said, rubbing his chin and looking baffled. This did not have the earmarks of an act. He really did look baffled. And yet he still did not name a destination.

I ran his body language and tone of voice through my Univac. It spat out a punch card that told me he was "up to something." I decided to try a ploy.

"Would you mind if I pulled into that McDonald's?" I said. "I always eat on the run when I drive a taxi, and I'd like to pick up some quick burgers."

"Oh that's fine, no problem, go right ahead, I'm in no hurry," Tony said, confirming what I believed—that we had never been going anywhere to begin with. This applies to a lot of things in life.

The McDonald's at Broadway and Alameda is a nice quiet out-of-the-way bistro that I sometimes patronize. When you're alone and hungry late at night on the mean streets of Denver, sometimes a hamburger in fifteen seconds is the only thing that keeps hope alive.

"The drive-up line is pretty long," I said. The drive-up lines are always long at McDonald's. The golden arch is a gold mine. Billions of burgers have been sold since its inception down in LA. Ray Kroc fascinates me.

"What say we step inside?" I said. "The lines always seem to be shorter for pedestrians."

He nodded.

There were only three people standing in line at the counter, but that's because Americans are programmed to remain inside their cars at all costs. I don't blame them. Cars cost a lot. You have to get as much use out of them as possible before they're recalled. My three favorite words are "possible," "plausible," and "probable" since they rarely apply to anything I do.

I paid and carried my load to the far end of the dining area. There were only two people at the tables, but I chose the booth nearest the restrooms. I wanted privacy. I wanted to be able to speak freely with Tony, but more importantly, I wanted Tony to be able to speak freely with me. And what fast-food consumer wants to eat near a toilet? I do. I always do.

I unwrapped a cheeseburger and went to work on it. Tony sat sipping at his coffee and looking out the picture window. The sun was streaming in where we sat. It felt good, which was strange, because I hate summer. Too hot. I hate winter, too, but for a different reason. I'm a spring and autumn man. Birth and death. Whatever happens in between doesn't interest me.

"I want to apologize again for not being at the shop yesterday," Tony said.

I nodded. I had lost count of how many times he had apologized to me for not being there. I wish more people would do that. Not be there I mean. Imagine the number of problems that have been caused in this world by people being somewhere.

"That's okay, Tony—if I may call you Tony."

He smiled and nodded, and took a quick sip of his coffee. He seemed nervous. I tried to think of the kinds of things that might make a barber nervous. A return of the long-hairs, I supposed, but that would make everybody nervous. The fact that I have long hair in no way clouds my objectivity. Being a professional fraud, I have spent the past forty-five years trying to figure out what's really going on at all times, since you don't know what you're faking until you know what's real. My desperate search for the truth occasionally has caused me embarrassment, but on the plus side it has left me virtually friendless.

"Gino told me you were at the shop for only a minute or so," Tony said. "He said you came in but left right away. He said you didn't hang around very long. That's right, isn't it? I mean … it didn't take you away from your driving, I hope."

I knew now that I was being interrogated, and it made sense. Tony had spent the entire morning looking for me. Why would anybody spend an entire morning looking for me unless he wanted to interrogate me? What else am I good for?

I set my burger down and looked Tony in the eye. "To tell you the truth," I lied, "I don't really know how long I was at your shop. After Gino told me you weren't there, we chatted for a bit."

"What did you talk about?" Tony said.

I picked up my Coke and stared into its depths. "I don't really remember," I said, which was sort of a lie and sort of a truth. This happens to me frequently.

There was a moment of awkward silence as I popped my last French fry into my mouth.

"Can I ask you a question, Murph?"

For the first time in fourteen years I suddenly didn't want to say yes to a paying customer.

"Yes."

"Did Gino mention my wife?"

It was rude, I suppose, but my jaw went slack, revealing a bit of deep-fried potato stuck to the surface of my tongue. I couldn't help it. The conversation had taken a sudden turn and was headed straight for Mars.

"I have something to tell you, Murph. When I got into your taxi on Monday, I wasn't there to meet my wife. I was hiding from my wife. I saw her coming out of the Hilton Hotel. I got into your taxi so she wouldn't see me."

Right past Mars and straight on to Jupiter.

I decided—about five minutes too late—that it was time for me to shut up.

I picked up my cup and let two ice cubes slide onto my tongue. This maneuver had something to do with nuns. When a nun asks you a question in arithmetic and you just sit there staring at her as if you were a guilt-wracked husband, you better have a good excuse. A mouthful of ice was the best I could come up with on short notice.

Tony raised his chin. "You see Murph, I was following my wife that day. I told my Uncle Gino that I was taking an early lunch, but I didn't eat lunch. I followed her downtown. At one point she went into the Hilton Hotel. I waited for ten minutes, and was about to follow her inside when I saw her coming out, so I jumped into your taxi."

By this time the ice was melted, and my tongue was frozen. I began to nod slowly. "I don't have the slightest idea why you're telling me these things, Tony."

Tony placed his right hand in front of his mouth the way you would to wipe away a milk mustache. He stared at me for five seconds, then lowered his hand and said, "One of the reasons I came looking for you this morning was to find out what you told my uncle. But there's another reason I came looking for you, Murph. I decided I wanted to ask something of you."

This was the worst news I'd had since Wichita. I make a special point of avoiding people who want to ask things of me. What makes anybody think I want to do things they don't want to do?

"Name it," I said.

He glanced down at the tabletop. "Hear me out before you agree to this. I know that you make your living driving a taxi, but I would be willing to pay you double your daily earnings if I could hire you to do something for me."

The word "double" hooked me like a rainbow trout. "I'm listening," I said.

"I would like to ask whether you might be willing to use your taxicab to follow my wife around town. I want to know where she goes."

Tony's eyes were darting from side to side, reading both of my eyes, which were rather large at the moment.

I suddenly heard a voice talking. It was mine. I listened closely. "This could cost you a lot, Tony. I pull in an average of one hundred and thirty dollars a day, part of which is my profits, and part of which goes to pay for a lease on my taxi and a tank of gas. Wouldn't it be more cost-efficient if you were to hire a private detective?"

"Oh God no," Tony said. "I don't want anything even vaguely resembling the law to be associated with this. I'll pay you a flat fee of three hundred dollars a day, if that's acceptable to you."

There comes a time in every man's life when common sense goes flying straight down the crapper, and this was one of them. The first thought that went through my mind was that if I dragged this thing out for a month I could make ninety thousand dollars. Then something told me I was wrong about that. A nun. I rechecked my figures, and it came to only nine thousand dollars. I felt like a writer calculating how much money he would get for a novel if he went commercial. As the nun's laughter faded from my mind, I had a more down-to-earth thought.

"How would I know when your wife leaves your house?" I said.

"She leaves the house every morning at eleven o'clock."

I picked up my paper cup and looked at the melted ice. I set it back down. "I'll be driving my taxi tomorrow," I said. "I suppose I could be in your neighborhood about that time."

Tony nodded. "What time do you go on duty?"

"I usually head out at seven in the morning."

"I'd like to pay you in advance," Tony said. "Could I meet you somewhere tomorrow morning? I don't want Gino to see us together, so it would have to be somewhere outside the barbershop."

For three hundred bucks it could be outside Cleveland. "How about a coffee shop?" I said.

Tony nodded. "Do you know The Busy Bee Cafe on east Colfax?"

I nodded. The Busy Bee has one of the cleanest restrooms in east Denver. Cabbies know the locations of all the public restrooms. I could write a book about the best restrooms in Denver if I wanted to write a book that nobody would buy. I've done that plenty of times.

"I could be there at nine A.M.," I said. "Would that work for you?"

Tony nodded. Meeting over.

We got up, walked outside, and climbed into 127. I drove Tony back to Broadway and Colfax. He was parked in a lot one block away from the Hilton. This time my meter was running. The fare came to six dollars. He gave me twelve.

Money is funny when you think about it. What is money anyway? I know what it is because I think about it a lot, in the way that starving men think about stomachs. Money is what we do instead of hunting wild boar. I don't know who he was, but I love the bastard who thought up money. I suspect it was somebody like me. Some Neanderthal named Moog who didn't want to come home to the cave with bleeding shins. God knows how he talked his pal Oog into going on the hunt for him. Oog must have badly wanted something that my ancestor Moog owned. A chicken, maybe. Or a flint spearhead. Or maybe Oog was just plain stupid. Maybe Oog was my ancestor. That made more sense. It would explain why my head was turned by the prospect of earning three hundred dollars a day for doing the one thing I had long ago vowed never to do again, which was to get involved in a fare's personal life.

After I dropped Tony off I decided to head down to the Fairmont Hotel again and check out the cab line. But it wasn't just that. Already I was trying to distance myself from the thing I had agreed to do. I was intentionally avoiding the Hilton, although this decision took place on a subconscious level. It was instinctive you might say, Pavlovian even, like the training I had undergone in the army where they had taught us to hit the dirt at the first sign of mops.

There were only two cabs at the Fairmont. I pulled up at the end of the line, shut everything down, sat back, and stared at my eyes in the mirror. They stared back at me. We looked at each other for a long time, until we came to the mutual conclusion that both of us were insane.

What if I ended up as a witness in a messy divorce case? If that happened, Hogan might find out that I was using my taxi to make money.

The first cab in line picked up a fare from the hotel. The other cabbie and I pulled forward.

What if I was spotted shadowing Tony's wife, and some gorilla dragged me out of my cab and threatened to punch me in the face? I had the sudden urge to buy glasses.

Another fare came out of the hotel and got into the cab ahead of me. I pulled forward and parked. I was alone at the cabstand. I felt like I had been alone at the cabstand all my life.

Suddenly I wanted out. I was just an ordinary Joe who had bitten off more than he could chew, lured by the siren song of a big score. Why did I ever drop out of KAU? If I had stayed in school I would be making little BA's right now, seeking tenure, and basking in the arms of Mary Margaret Flaherty every night. I was a fool.

A well-dressed man carrying a suitcase came out of the Fairmont. He looked pleased with himself, was grinning. He looked like he had successfully closed a business deal and was on his way home. He climbed into my backseat and said, "Airport." But my heart did not soar like an eagle. My teeth did not clench with pleasure. I dropped my flag, turned on the meter, and pulled away from the curb.

The thrill was gone.

CHAPTER 10

I was right. All the way to the airport the businessman talked about a deal he had just closed with a real estate developer. I had to dig down deep to pretend to be happy for him, which was a shame because I really was happy for him. He was like a guy I knew back in college who once sold a short story to a literary magazine. When someone you know makes it, you're happy for him, even though you're jealous. His success means there's still hope. It's a shame that hope hinges on success. Why can't hope hinge on failure? Think how successful everybody would be.

After I dropped my fare off I drove over to the cabstand at DIA to see if it would be worth my time to wait for a trip back to Denver instead of deadheading. The cabstand is an island of asphalt in a weed field, a staging area where the cabbies wait for their turn to make the long winding drive up to the terminal, which looks like an avant-garde circus tent. I decided not to hang around the airport.

I was on the scene the first day DIA opened for business. Every cab driver in Denver was edgy. What was this going to do for the taxi business? When I showed up that first morning, there were practically no cabs in line. The bulk of the drivers were staying away until they found out how things were shaping up. In four hours I made three runs. A hundred and fifty bucks and I still had eight hours to go. I was in pig heaven.

But by noon The Word was out. Pretty soon almost every cabbie in Denver showed up, except Big Al. He said DIA was going to ruin the cab business. There must have been two hundred taxis in line. I freaked. The dream was dying. As the days went by and things fell into a pattern, the average waiting time to get out of the staging area was three hours, and that was on a good day. Sometimes it was five hours. The best I could ever manage out of DIA was two trips. I went back to jumping bells and working hotels.

When I got back to downtown Denver I took a few calls off the radio, but because my mind was on other things, the dispatcher yelled at me. I had forgotten an address on Capitol Hill. First time in years. This wounded my cabbie ego. I decided to sit out the rest of my shift at hotels. I went to the Brown Palace and found Big Al at his tip-sheet, scoping out the dogs. I walked up to his cab and tapped on his roof.

He glanced at me and shook his head. "You made the dispatcher's shit list today didn'tcha, cherry boy? How many times did I tell you to write down addresses?"

Not enough, rough estimate. Big Al was a good taxi teacher. I was not so good a student. But this had always been true. From the moment I entered first grade I had school pegged as a hoax. Twelve years later I was still convinced. I lost interest fast. I spent most of my youth staring out windows at the playground and wondering what was so fascinating about baseball.

"How are you making out with the dogs?" I said to change the subject from shit lists to something I knew less about.

"I can loan you a pen and notebook if you need one, Tenderfoot," Big Al said. Big Al was like a pit bull. Once he got his teeth into you, it would take more than amateurish evasion to make him turn loose.

"Ricky Rocket never made it off the launching pad, did he?" I said. That was a cruel thing to say, but I was in a cruel mood.

"I can't win for losing," Big Al sighed, his armor cracking. Now I felt bad. He lowered the tip-sheet and looked up at me. "Come clean," he said. "When I heard the dispatcher yell at you, I got worried. What's the problem?"

"Aaagh," I said, standing away from his cab and looking toward the doorway to the Brown. "Three no-shows in a row."

He didn't believe me. His eyes gave him away. But he let loose of it and just nodded. No-shows are the bane of an asphalt warrior's existence. People call for a cab and then aren't home when you knock. As good an excuse as any for saying, "Aaagh." Big Al understood that I didn't want to talk.

But I did. I wanted to talk bad. Real bad. I wanted to tell him that I had made a mistake. But I couldn't. He had been my mentor. I didn't want to disappoint him twice in one day. But I knew what he would say if I came clean. "Don't ask me for pity, chump. Just ride it out and pray for a miracle."

A fare walked out of the Brown. The line of cabs came to life and began driving forward one space. I went back to my cab and got in, but instead of pulling forward I wheeled out onto the street and drove away. I headed back to the Hilton. I decided that if Tony was hanging out there I would cancel the deal. This had been a mistake from the get-go. Spying on a woman was leaving a bad taste in my mouth. It reminded me of the time I stole ten dollars from the Eagle Scout.

All right. Here's my Eagle Scout story:

I was ten years old. I was a Tenderfoot in the Boy Scouts. Camp Wa-Ni-Ta-Ka. They made us do handicrafts. They made us sleep in two-man tents. They made us hike in the woods. By the second day I wanted to crawl right out of my own skin. I had five days left to go and I was broke. I had gone through the two dollars my Maw had given me for "spending money." Yeah. As if there's any other kind of money.

Camp Wa-Ni-Ta-Ka had a little log cabin in the middle of the grounds. They called it the Trading Post. It was like a rustic 7/11.

It sold Coke, candy bars, Eskimo Pies, the works. If you were flush, you could buy a leather kit to make a belt, or a block of wood to carve a neckerchief slide. But I wasn't flush. Two hours after I climbed off the bus on Sunday afternoon I had blown my wad on Eskimo Pies. I got a bellyache that night. It was the best bellyache I ever had.

On Tuesday they made us row boats. I was with three other scouts. The scoutmasters ordered us to take turns rowing around the lake. But I told a scout named Nick that I would allow him to take my turn if he paid me a dime. He fell for it. Who the hell wanted to row a damn boat? Nick did. One dime could buy two Eskimo Pies back in the days when a nickel was worth a dollar, adjusted for inflation. I couldn't wait to get back to the dock.

While Nick was getting red in the face yanking our boat all over the lake, I glanced around at the flat Kansas landscape trying to work up a woodsy feeling. I was trapped there for a week, I was down to my last dime, and I was ready to capitulate. These were my formative years.

Then I saw something lying on the bottom of the boat. I was sitting in the pointy part of the boat. What do sailors call it? The prow? Don't ask me. I served in the army. But I could spot a billfold a mile away. I can still do that. The billfold must have fallen out of the back pocket of some kid.

I casually reached down and surreptitiously pocketed the billfold, then I began whining. I told the other scouts my belly ached and I wanted to go to the Red Cross cabin. They bitched. They moaned. They called me a doofus. But I got my way. I can still do that.

After they dropped me off I took a little hike into the woods. The trees were thick, crowded, probably the only cluster in Kansas. I opened the billfold and examined the I.D. card. It belonged to Chauncey Roqueforte, Eagle Scout, the highest-ranking scout in our troop—Troop 42, Blessed Virgin Catholic Grade School, Archdiocese of Wichita, Monsignor Michael O'Leary presiding.

Then I opened the cash pocket and looked right into the eyes of mister sawbuck himself: Alexander Hamilton. My mouth went dry. I began reciting the twelve points of the Scout Law: trustworthy, loyal, helpful, friendly, courteous, kind, obedient, cheerful, thrifty, brave, clean, reverent. It was a wash. I pocketed the ten and buried the billfold beneath a pile of leaves at the base of a tree.

That evening I staggered back to my tent bloated with Eskimo Pies and sucking on a bottle of Coke. The rest of the week was a blur. When the other scouts were seated around a campfire listening to Indian lore, I was seated on the wooden steps of the Trading Post gaining weight. Ten dollars could buy two hundred ice-cream bars in those days.

By Friday night I was down to my last quarter. I was lying in my tent coming off the world's greatest sugar high when I heard a bunch of kids hollering. One word in particular caught my attention: billfold! I crawled off my cot and staggered to the flap. I opened it and stepped outside and saw a group of young, healthy, tanned, robust Catholics standing around a scoutmaster and waving something I could spot a mile away.

"We found a billfold in the woods!"

I eased back into my tent.

I placed one ear against the flap and listened as the scouts explained how they had discovered the billfold beneath a pile of leaves at the base of a tree in the middle of the woods. Fer the luvva Christ.

I decided to make myself scarce.

I exited through the rear of my tent and headed for the Trading Post to knock back a snow pie and try to forget. But then I stopped. They might be watching the snack bar. They might be watching the roads. I began to sweat. I fled across a field toward the lake where I threw myself to the ground and gazed up at the stars. I knew they would come looking for me. They always came looking for me. Every time the scouts lined up to DO something, a scoutmaster would shout, "Where the hell's that lazy kid!"

My heart was pounding. The scoutmasters were probably interrogating every boy in the camp right now. I would be the only one missing. They would know.

I got up and trudged back to camp, slipped into the rear of my tent, lay down on my cot, and waited.

And waited. And waited.

Strangely, nothing came of it. I got off scot-free.

Or did I?

An elderly couple came out of the Hilton Hotel. I was the first cab in line by then. I cruised up to the door, but it wasn't until I climbed out to open my trunk that I realized it was the two rubes from Chicago.

"Well hello again!" the woman said, flashing me a dazzling grin.

"Howdy there, young fella," the man said. "We're going to the airport."

I got rattled. I put their suitcases into the trunk, but remained at the rear until Francois escorted them into the backseat of my taxi. I gently closed the lid and walked toward the driver's door. I wanted to keep on walking. I wanted to walk all the way to Camp Wa-Ni-Ta-Ka and throw myself on the mercy of Lord Baden-Powell, the founder of the Boy Scouts.

Instead, I climbed into the driver's seat and started the engine, hit the meter, and pulled out. We would be together for half an hour. My only hope was to recall the plot of *The Three Faces of Eve* and try to become Joanne Woodward. It worked.

"How was your stay in Denver?" I chirped.

"Oh, we had a wonderful time," the woman said, patting the back of her hair.

"Marvelous, just marvelous," her husband said.

"But you know," the woman said, tilting her head and frowning, "we missed the gunfight down at Larimer Square. We were sooo disappointed. I was hoping to take a picture for my grandchildren."

Somehow I managed not to flip out. I drove to the airport and dropped them off at the terminal. They gave me fifty-five dollars. I got out of there fast.

By the time my shift ended I had made two airport runs, had lied to an elderly couple, got yelled at by the dispatcher, and sold my soul to the devil. It was time to go home and tote up my profits.

CHAPTER 11

My civilian car is a two-door, two-tone 1964 Chevy. The two tones are black and red. The doors are red, the rest of the body is black. The doors are red because that was the only color I could find at the junk-yard after my car was stripped.

I live on Capitol Hill. It is neither the best nor the worst part of Denver. My apartment is a few blocks from Cheesman Park. The site of my building stands on a kind of dividing line between broke Denver and rich Denver.

By "broke" I mean young people who go to college, have crappy jobs, live two or more to an apartment, and are on their way up in the world, living the kind of bohemian life on the west end of "The Hill" that most young people are forced to live when they first leave home: beatnik, hippie, punk, whatever—the kind of life I led in a big chunk of American cities after I left Wichita.

The rich live east of The Hill. By "rich" I think you know what I mean. If you have to ask, you can't afford to.

My Chevy gets stolen every now and then from the parking lot of the apartment building where I live. It doesn't stay stolen long though. When the vermin who hot-wire it finally figure out what they're driving, they abandon it. The first time it got stolen years ago I was apoplectic with rage. Two hours later a cop knocked on my door and told me my car was sitting in the parking lot of a grocery store on east Colfax.

I like cops. They give me back my car.

About eight years ago my heap was stolen for the nineteenth time, and after the cop told me where it was, I discovered that the thieves had removed my doors. I asked the cop if it was legal to drive a car without doors, and he said yes, there was no law against it. It was like a jeep. For a week I drove my Chevy around Denver doorless, just to show the bastards they couldn't get me down. They finally got me down. I went to a few junkyards, but all I could find were red doors.

My parking space is in a corner of the lot where two wooden fences converge creating a ninety-degree V. "The V Spot" is the choice space in the lot. I've lived in the building longer than any of the other tenants, so I sort of graduated to it. When I first moved in I had the space closest to the street. That's where my car got stolen most often. As I moved closer to the V over the years, the rate diminished. I've had my car stolen only three times since I became boss-hog of the dirt lot.

It was still light out when I got home that night. The solstice had passed and the days were getting shorter. I once read an article about an experiment where a man lived in a subterranean cavern for six months and his biological clock went on a 25-hour day. Just think of it. A person can live longer by totally avoiding the surface of the earth.

That's where I wanted to be right then. On the moon. I parked my heap in the private dirt lot behind my building and trudged the three flights up the fire escape to the back door of my crow's nest, thinking about the job I had agreed to do for Tony. I had almost forgotten what it was like to have an obligation. I had abandoned the concept of obligations on the day I walked out of Dyna-Plex.

All right. Here's what I did at Dyna-Plex:

I wrote brochures. When I had told the UCD student that half of my English major buddies were corporate writers, I really meant me. That's what broke me. I could never figure out what the Dyna-Plex Corporation's business consisted of, i.e., I wasn't sure how they made money. None of the executives I interviewed seemed to know either. It may have had something to do with plastic skylights, or else oil-shale leases. I considered calling the SEC to find out if they knew, but I had seen enough Jack Lemmon movies to know not to make waves. As long as the bank cashed my paycheck every month, I minded my own business. As far as I could tell, the job of most of the employees was to empty the water coolers twice an hour.

Anyway, when I got home that night I dropped my cab accoutrement onto the kitchen table and went into the living room. I turned on the TV just to have some noise while I fixed a hamburger. I went through the motions of preparing the burger like an automaton. This is what happens to me when I undertake an obligation. I become fixated by the idea that I have to DO something that I don't want to do. Of course I never want to do anything. That's why I drive a taxi.

Even though the TV was on, and even though Mary Ann was winsomely teasing Gilligan, I sat down at the kitchen table with my burger and ate it with a beer. Third burger of the day. After I left Wichita I ate hamburgers morning, noon, and night. My Maw would have brought the curse of the banshee down on my head if she knew I ate hamburgers for breakfast. In her opinion, eating hamburgers for breakfast was the first step on the slippery slope to rowdyism. Maybe she was right.

Suddenly I wanted to be back home in Wichita. I wanted to be ten years old again. I wanted Maw to fix me free meals again. She didn't start charging me for meals until I got a paper route, which lasted a month. Then she put me on a tab.

I call my Maw twice a year and don't ask for money. She set me straight on that issue after I got a job passing out leaflets in Pittsburgh. "Don't look to me for pity, chump," she said. My Maw and Big Al have a lot in common.

After Gilligan ended I shut off the TV, which is rare for me. I started feeling edgy again. Obligations do this to me. I really do not have much experience with obligations, which might explain why they affect me this way. Maybe if I painted myself into more corners I would have some expertise to draw upon, but I spent my adult life avoiding obligations. The army had something to do with this. Two years of making my bed every morning was a grind. I thought the army would be more like an Ian Fleming novel. I suppose that, technically speaking, all soldiers are licensed to kill, but my army career involved killing time. I realize that my use of the word "career" might sound pretentious, but if I'm forced to do anything for more than two weeks I lose all perspective.

Suddenly I started thinking about those dusty dumbbells in my closet. I tried not to think about the ThighMaster. I felt the urge to drag the dumbbells out and do some curls. I needed a release from the psychological tic that was beleaguering my mind. The army had something to do with this, too. Whenever we were ordered to do physical training exercises, such as pushups or jumping jacks, I found that it cleared my mind. Maybe "too exhausted to think" is a better way of putting it. I'll be honest, I actually enjoyed PT training. I looked forward to anything that made me stop thinking about the fact that I had to perform jumping jacks for two years.

I got up and went to my closet, opened the door, and started to reach down for the dumbbells. But then I stopped. I took a moment to go find a whisk broom to sweep off the weights before I picked them up. Do you have any idea how much dust can accumulate in a single spot over a period of fourteen years? It's quite impressive.

I had bought the dumbbells on the same day that I was hired to drive for RMTC. On the way home that night I realized that driving a cab would not simply entail sitting, it would also involve hoisting luggage into trunks. I hadn't thought about that when I decided to apply for the job, and by the time the true horror of what I had done to myself hit me, it was too late. I had already paid $25.00 for my DOT physical. I guess you could say I had painted myself into a corner.

I passed a Salvation Army store that day. I shop at Salvation Army stores a lot. T-shirts go for a song at SA, although it's difficult to find T-shirts that have a breast pocket, which is crucial for a cabbie. An asphalt warrior needs immediate access to his money. You don't want to take your customer's mind off his tip by digging around in your jeans looking for change. But I suspect that most fares say, "Keep the change," because they don't want to touch things that have been dug out of my pants. That's just a theory, but it's probably true.

I stopped in at SA that day because I knew they sold used athletic equipment—I frequently bypassed the athletic corner on my way to the bookshelves. I collect used books, but let's keep moving. If you have ever shopped at SA you know that sale items come and go fast, so you never know what you might find. On that day I had a choice between an Olympic bench press fully equipped with barbells, or else two twenty-pound dumbbells. They both came cheap, but I didn't think I had enough room for the bench press in my Chevy or in my life, so I opted for the dumbbells. I wanted to exercise only the muscles that I would use to lift luggage. But first I took the dumbbells for a test drive.

I picked them up and hefted them in my fists. They felt just like suitcases. I practiced walking around the store with them. Pretty soon I noticed two guys following me. They looked like truck drivers. The manager of the SA finally asked if I intended to make a purchase. I said yes, and the two men returned to the back room where they started unloading ThighMasters from the rear of a Salvation Army truck backed up to the loading door. Don't let me mislead you though. I did not buy my ThighMaster at SA. I don't want to talk about it.

When I went to pay for the dumbbells I almost set them on the glass-topped display case where the cash register was located. By "almost" I mean I didn't. That was a minor miracle, given the fact that exercise empties my mind. I set them on the floor, then stood up and smiled at the cashier who looked about seventeen years old. She smiled back at me and said, "Do you qualify for the senior citizen's discount, sir?"

That was the day my world ended.

I told her no. I paid and stormed angrily out of the place. It was only after I hoisted the dumbbells into the trunk of my car that I realized I should have said yes. Fer the luvva Christ, I could have saved a buck. Even if she had checked my I.D. and found out I wasn't a member of A.A.R.P., what could she have done to me? Called the S.W.A.T. team? Phoned my Maw? So I guess my mind was empty after all, at least the financial acumen part. I've always been lousy at math.

Let's get this over with.

The night I brought the dumbbells home from SA I did three sets of curls and never touched them again. Does this story have a familiar ring? Don't be embarrassed. At least you don't own a ThighMaster.

Or do you?

After I finished cleaning the dumbbells with the whisk broom I began choking on the cloud of dust. I was forced to slam the door shut and forget about exercising. The activity involved in whisking, combined with my memory of how I came to possess those weights, cured me of my psychological tic. That may have been the best two bucks I ever spent at SA.

Due to the fact that there were no Gilligan episodes being shown on cable, I decided to kill the rest of the evening working on a novel. This is a game writers play. They pretend they can write novels only if every other conceivable activity in the entire universe has been taken care of. God forbid there should be a dirty dish in the house that might distract them from their productivity. I have a theory that the word "productivity" is a contraction of "production" and "activity." It was probably coined by Henry Ford, although I have no proof—yet. But who else would waste his time inventing more efficient ways of saying things fast than a time management expert?

Okay. I'll be honest. I went into the kitchen and did the dish before I opened my steamer trunk and began digging through my old manuscripts.

I pulled out an old coffee-stained manuscript titled "The Invulnerable Man." This was another college try. Unfinished, of course. It was the story of a twenty-year-old kid who was invulnerable. He didn't have super powers. He couldn't fly or see through walls. He was just invulnerable. He couldn't be hurt physically. You could tie his ass to an atom bomb and set it off, and he would get tossed ten miles into the air, land on the ground, and walk away. That's not only a description of his physiology, it's also the plot. I don't know how he got to be invulnerable. Probably a laboratory experiment gone awry. I didn't waste my time in college worrying about cause or motivation in my fiction. I was concerned primarily with symbolism. That was during my Sartre period. I was convinced that the character's invulnerability was symbolic of something or other, if only I could figure out what. Most of the story consisted of the kid sitting under a tree watching traffic go by and contemplating how unusual it was to be invulnerable.

I put the pages back into the steamer trunk and closed the lid. I went into the bedroom, switched off the lights, kicked off my Keds, and collapsed into bed. I had an onerous obligation hanging over my head and it completely drained me of the will to write, thank God.

It's a funny thing about sleep. It's like a garbage disposal. You go to bed with your mind cluttered with dismal thoughts, and you wake up feeling as if your brain has been rinsed and repeated. Maybe it's the dreams. No matter how bad your thoughts are as you drift off to sleep, nothing can compare with the psychotic comedy of nocturnal TV. Maybe the function of dreaming is to bring in the professional dramatists to show you just how lame your conscious imagination is, to put everything into perspective, to make mincemeat out of your so-called personal problems. I won't bore you with the dreams I had that night, the barking skeleton on the roller coaster, etc. To me, the fascinating thing about dreams is how utterly boring they are to other people. You can wake up from a dream weirder than high school and try to describe it to your friends, and you end up putting them to sleep. The greatest writer who ever lived, whoever he was, could never accurately capture in words the surreal landscapes, the bizarre atmospherics, and the twisted emotions generated by that pot roast lodged between everybody's ears.

Neither can I. All I can say is, I woke up Thursday morning feeling like three hundred bucks. Whatever had been eating me alive the night before apparently had been eaten by that barking skeleton. I came to consciousness thinking about the prospect of earning more than two day's worth of profits in one day for doing what I do best: sitting down.

The sky was clear, the day was destined to be warm, and as I fried my breakfast burger I made a few rough plans: pick up my cab, grab a cup of coffee at 7-11, make a couple runs from the Brown, then head east to the Busy Bee Cafe and pocket three bills. Follow a woman around town for a couple of hours, maybe hoof it occasionally, then report back to Tony. Home by six, a romp in the sand with Mary Ann, and so to bed.

By then I realized that this chore was not going to last a month. I doubted I would even be doing it the following day. I drove my heap to Rocky and parked in the dirt lot. I walked into the on-call room and let Rollo know I was there. Cab #127 was still on the road, so there would be a wait. This was not unusual. A newbie driver had pulled a night shift in 127 and was probably frantically trying to figure out why he hadn't made a dime.

Sheila walked through the room carrying a manila folder. She glanced at me and stopped.

"Hogan has seen your DOT physical," she said. "He knows you need glasses. Did you buy new ones yet?"

I thought about lying to Sheila. But I couldn't do it. I don't mean I wasn't capable, or even unwilling, I just mean that lying to Sheila would have been as successful as lying to my Maw. My Maw and Sheila have a lot in common.

"No," I said.

She hoisted her eyebrows above the rims of her big red girl-glasses and said, "Mm hmmm." That said it all. "Do you intend to take care of it today?"

"Yes," I lied.

"Mm hmmm." She reached into the pocket of her flowery dress and pulled out a pair of girl-glasses made with ordinary black rims. "You be wearing these if Hogan comes around. It doesn't mean nothing to me, Murph, but I suggest you get your act together by tomorrow."

That was a mighty tall order in more ways than one.

I thanked Sheila for her concern, then spent a few minutes resenting the fact that she could read me like an X-ray.

The newbie finally came into the on-call room looking like Rod Taylor in the opening scene of *The Time Machine*. He staggered over to the cage, handed the key to Rollo, and staggered back out the door. I never saw him again.

I took the key and a trip-sheet from Rollo and headed out to the lot, suddenly concerned that 127 might look like the newbie. I checked it for dings and dents but didn't find any. I checked the backseat for vomit. The drunks come out of the bars at two A.M. and a lot of things come out of the drunks. You name it, I've hosed it down.

But the seat was clean. The poor kid probably hadn't even earned back his lease payment for the night—not unlike my first night shift. I got in and noted that there was still half a tank of gas on the gauge. Tough break for the kid. He probably had sat outside hotels all night praying for a miracle. The night shift is a specialty act. Midnight to six A.M. is fairly dead, so you have to learn where the zombies walk. I generally avoid pulling night shifts unless I have something special planned for the daylight hours, like sleeping.

I stopped at 7-11 for a joe and a Twinkie, but I didn't gas up. I knew I could make it through the day without needing a full tank. As soon as I reported back to Tony that afternoon, I planned to turn in my cab rather than pull a full shift, then head home for spring break.

CHAPTER 12

A nd now for a little angst.

I got settled in at the cabstand by the Brown Palace around seven thirty, but then it occurred to me that I might get an airport run that morning, which could bollix my scheduled meeting with Tony at nine. Even though the Busy Bee was in east Denver, it would still be cutting it thin if I found myself headed out to DIA at eight o'clock. I began to be concerned about time. I began to fret about my schedule. Suddenly I found my stomach being tied in knots by the clock!

Let me tell you something about clocks.

When you've been driving a taxi as long as I have, you become a time master. You're like a quarterback managing the clock during the last two minutes of a football game. You run the clock, the clock doesn't run you. The crux of the matter is always money, like the numbers on the scoreboard above the goal post. But if you've only earned thirty bucks profit for the day and there's forty minutes left until your shift is over, you pause a minute and take a breather to decide whether it's worth it to try for one more fare, or to just call it a day, take your thirty bucks home and shove it in your *Finnegans Wake*. There's always tomorrow. That's the thing. That's why you're never a slave to the clock. There's always tomorrow.

But a scheduled meeting? That takes the football out of your hands. The pigskin becomes the elephant in the living room of your life. You have to work around it. Every move you make has to be measured against the obligation that you shouldered like an idiot. In the world of in-house corporate writing they call it a deadline. That's one of the many reasons I walked out of Dyna-Plex. They did things by the clock. That may sound like an efficient way to run a business—but can it truly be said that there is an efficient way to do meaningless things? In other words, what's the difference between competent meaninglessness and incompetent meaninglessness?

Every week at Dyna-Plex the employees had to take part in the Monday Morning Meeting. The boss would go around the table asking everybody what they were working on, and they would give a report. I always told him I was making headway on "the brochure." He would tell all of us to keep up the good work. The meeting would break up and most of the employees would begin draining jugs. I would go to my desk and light a cigarette. This was back in the days when you could commit suicide indoors without getting fined by the EPA. I would pick up a #2 pencil and begin scribbling meaningless phrases on a yellow legal pad such as "more bang for your buck" or "reinvent the wheel" or "work smarter, not harder." People thought I was working on "the brochure." Every month I was required to produce one brochure for Dyna-Plex, and I was given a deadline.

The word deadline is defined as "a boundary line in a prison that prisoners can cross only at the risk of being shot." I looked that up in my *American Heritage Dictionary* one afternoon at Dyna-Plex. Apparently, if I didn't complete the brochure by the last day of the month I would be gunned down. The prospect of becoming a crumpled corpse was the only thing about my job that intrigued me.

I don't know what Dyna-Plex did with those brochures, how they were distributed, or who read them. I know only that the brochures contained absolutely no practical information whatsoever because I had no idea what Dyna-Plex did to make money.

It suddenly occurred to me that I had no business waiting in front of the Brown Palace on a day when I was going to rake in three hundred dollars. In all probability I would have earned only twenty dollars making a couple of runs from the Brown before going to see Tony. So why did I even consider it? By now you ought to know the answer: more money.

Money is always the crux. Three hundred and twenty dollars for the day had a better ring to it than three hundred. But I realized it was pointless to try to pick up a few more crumbs—and an airport run could jeopardize my deadline. Sometimes you just have to do things before you realize how stupid they are.

I started my engine and pulled out of line at the Brown without a fare. In doing so, I pulled myself out from beneath the clock. I ceased to worry about airport runs. I ceased to worry about time. I became a time master.

It was a quarter to eight. I drove over to Colfax and began cruising east, no longer concerned about the clock. I had more than an hour to go before the meeting at the Busy Bee. I knew I could dawdle, the one thing my Maw had forbidden me to do since I was five years old. Nuns were also heavily into not dawdling. One of my dreams as a boy was to get my high school diploma, leave home, and start dawdling. That was the only dream that ever came true.

I crossed over Colorado Boulevard and entered the business district of east Colfax, the land of used cars and liquor stores, and only now did the onerous nature of my obligation begin to creep back. I glanced at my wristwatch, a quarterback working the minutes, working the pigskin, working the damned Oakland Raiders. Time appeared to be slowing down. But I was familiar with this phenomenon. Whenever I had a job that I wanted to get shut of, the universe seemed to catch wind of it and began tapping its brakes and slowing down. I would prefer to think that my brain was actually speeding up, but I doubt if I could get a consensus on that.

Relativity bugs me.

I cruised past the Busy Bee Cafe. People were going in and out the door, shopkeepers, truck drivers, blue-collar workers, the kinds of people I was when I had real jobs. I kept driving east. I passed Gino's Barbershop but kept looking straight ahead. I began fantasizing about driving all the way to Kansas like a long-haul taxi driver going clear to the East Coast. I wondered if any cabbie had ever gone nuts and done something like that. If a driver did pull a stunt like that, he would probably capture the public's imagination like in *The Sugarland Express*. As he passed through small towns, people would cheer him on and throw tips at him. I occasionally have dreams where I go down to Rocky Cab, climb into a taxi, and drive away without signing in or getting a trip-sheet. As I drive the unauthorized taxi around Denver, I feel a gleeful sense of evil knowing that I'm going to get caught and not caring. I wonder if that's symbolic of something.

I finally circled back and headed west on Colfax. There was still half an hour left when I finally parked my cab at the curb. I sat there for a while, thinking about taking up smoking again. I used to love sipping a cup of hot coffee and smoking a cigarette at dawn back at Dyna-Plex. But I decided against it. I got out of my cab and entered the Busy Bee, sat down on a stool at the counter, and ordered a Coke and a croissant.

The waitress at the Busy Bee knew me from previous visits. Her name was Millie. She was young. She was pretty. She was single. Her favorite color was blue. You get to know all the waitresses in all the cafes that have first-class restrooms. After Millie set my order down in front of me, she reached under the counter and pulled out a long block of wood with a key dangling from it. She held it up.

"No thanks, Millie," I said, waving it off with an appreciative smile.

She raised her eyebrows with surprise, then put the lumber back in its place.

Tony walked in at nine o'clock on the dot. He looked like he had slept badly the night before, yet he had a kind of watery, hopeful look in his eyes. He smiled at me and nodded. He was wearing a white smock beneath a longish jacket. The barbershop was six blocks farther east. Tony seemed a little out of breath as he said good morning. He ordered a cup of coffee from Millie.

"My uncle expects me back within half an hour," he said quietly.

I nodded.

"How do you want to work this?" I said.

Tony took a sip from his cup, set it down and looked me in the eye. "I'll ride with you back toward the shop. You can let me out a block away. We'll talk during the ride."

We finished our drinks. I swallowed the last bit of my croissant and stood up from the counter. Tony grabbed the check and went to the cash register. As I was heading for the door I heard a woman's voice call out, "Hey, cabbie, did you forget something?"

I turned and saw Millie standing behind the counter holding the restroom key above her head.

I shook my head no. "Catch you next time, sweetheart," I said with a wink. I walked out the door.

Tony came out as I was getting settled in the driver's seat. He carried himself like an ordinary guy merely coming out of a coffee shop and getting into a taxi. Things were running smoothly. I started the engine, dropped my flag, hit the meter, and pulled away from the curb. Just an ordinary cabbie hauling an ordinary fare. As we headed toward Gino's, Tony leaned forward and placed both hands on the seatback the way old men kneel in church: the sit/kneel. "Are you absolutely certain you want to go through with this?" he said.

How many times had I asked myself that question since I was ten? Well—how many grains of sand are there on the beach? I'm talking old math and not that New Math junk.

"I'm fine with it, Tony," I said in a voice so calm and confident that I couldn't figure out who I was imitating. Maybe it was me. I had never tried that before.

"I want to thank you for doing this, Murph," he said, but before I could explain how he could give me a proper thanks, he reached inside his pocket and withdrew a long white envelope.

Thick.

Almost as thick as my voice when I took it from his hand and croaked, "Thanks." I slipped it into the plastic briefcase lying open at my side.

Tony told me his home address. It was farther east, on a side street off 17th Avenue, way, way east of the dividing line on the The Hill where I planned to inaugurate my double spring break that evening. Tony told me that his wife, Angelina, ought to be leaving the house at eleven o'clock, just as she had every day for the past couple of weeks. His voice sort of faded as he said this. I thought about asking whether he himself wanted to go through with it, but the envelope told me to clam up. I gently closed the lid on the briefcase and said I was going to turn down a side street. We were a block away from Gino's.

I parked at the curb. Tony told me that if there were any problems I should give him a call at the shop. "Do you still have my card?" he said.

I tapped my briefcase with a fingernail and nodded.

"My Uncle Gino always leaves work at five o'clock," Tony said. "I plan to stay late. I'll tell him I'm going to work on the books. Whatever you find out, give me a call after five. I'll be alone in the shop."

"I'll give you a call at exactly a quarter after," I said.

I hoped Tony wouldn't reach across the seatback and try to shake my hand—it's awkward as hell to do that when you're seated behind a steering wheel. But he just said thanks again and opened the door and climbed out. I watched in the rear-view mirror as he jogged back toward Colfax. He turned at the corner and slowed to a normal pace and disappeared beyond the corner of a liquor store.

I glanced down at the closed lid of the briefcase. I wanted to yank it open and rifle the envelope to see the bundle of cash in person, but it was time to go—literally. I put 127 into gear and sped back to the Busy Bee. I really had to pee.

CHAPTER 13

Angelina came out the door at eleven o'clock. Based on what little information I had already gleaned, both Tony and his wife appeared to be slaves to the elephant. That was probably a good thing. I admire people who are reliable. Not envy, just admire.

My cab was parked three houses down. I had arrived five minutes earlier and spent four minutes pretending to be a cab driver, which I am good at. I got out and opened my trunk as if expecting a fare to come out of a nearby house. I went back to the driver's door and reached in and picked up the microphone and pretended to talk into it. I did cabbie things. I blended with the landscape. At one minute to eleven I shut the trunk and climbed back into the driver's seat and crossed my fingers hoping that Tony was right, even though I was hoping that Tony was wrong. I wanted to do this thing and I didn't want to do it. But like I always say, when laziness collides with cash, count me in.

The door to Tony's house opened. A woman emerged carrying a purse. I heard a strange and distant ringing in my ears. Angelina's dress was the type that lady executives wear. Coat. Tie. Skirt. It made me think of Dyna-Plex. I blocked that from my mind and focused. Mrs. Bombalini crossed the lawn and climbed into a gray Mercedes parked in the driveway. I made a mental note to become a barber.

After the Mercedes backed out and headed down the street, I started 127 and pulled away from the curb. The ringing got stronger in my ears. I knew the source: responsibility. My body responds to responsibility the way most mammals respond to imminent danger, or else sex. Bells were going off inside my head. My blood pressure was mounting. It had been years since I had undertaken a job that might be loosely defined as "important." It was like learning how to walk again.

But I had no problem tailing the Mercedes. I cruised along thinking how convenient it was that I drove a car that looked like scores of cars on the road, some of which passed us going both ways. Taxis make good camouflage.

It took twenty minutes to get to downtown Denver, and by that time the thrill of the hunt had faded. I merely felt like a taxi driver following someone. Reality had set in. I kind of liked it. The ringing had stopped. It had been replaced by curiosity. I followed her to the intersection of 15th Street, where she turned off and began driving toward the skyscrapers.

For those of you unfamiliar with this burg, downtown Denver is laid out at angles to the north-south vectors of the earth—meaning it's crooked. The pioneers who settled this part of the West apparently didn't own compasses. This may explain why they ended up in Denver instead of Sutter's Mill. The streets of Denver run parallel to the bed of the Platte River, which runs at an angle to the hemispheric latitudes. If you look at Denver on a map, the downtown area looks like a crooked shingle lying on a tiled floor. The easterners who arrived after the damage was done began laying out the streets north-south, east-west. My theory is that the new immigrants were angry taxi drivers, but I don't have any solid evidence ... yet. I can only tell you that the screwed-up pattern of the downtown streets makes them a pain to navigate. Finding an address can be a nightmare for a newbie cabbie or a newbie resident.

I turned onto the angle of 15th Street and followed Mrs. Bombalini to a parking lot. She pulled in and parked in a slot. I cruised past and watched as she climbed out and went to a big red metal box to pay for the slot.

Rather than park and follow Mrs. Bombalini on foot, I doubled around the block and watched from my cab as she made her way across 15th Street and entered the Strand Building, a new skyscraper that stood where an old one had stood when I first came to Denver. Most of nineteenth-century Denver has disappeared in the downtown area. It was demolished and replaced with glass walls that tended to blind vehicular traffic during the morning and evening rush hours. But I doubt if the architects cared. Architects strike me as a rather egocentric horde, concerned primarily with making their reputations and getting the hell out of Denver, sort of like local rock bands.

I pulled over to the curb and waited in a no-parking zone, keeping an eye out for cops. This is one of the virtually nonexistent benefits of driving a taxi. As long as you remain inside your cab and look like you're waiting for a fare to come out of a building, the cops will leave you alone. You could damn near park on top of the mayor's nephew and the cops wouldn't tell you to move along, provided you stayed inside your cab. But if you walk into a building, it becomes just another ticket magnet. I stayed in my taxi until Mrs. Bombalini walked out, looking slightly disheveled.

I slowly reached into my briefcase and pulled out the black-rimmed girl-glasses that Sheila had given me. I slid them on. They became my "disguise."

Mrs. Bombalini pulled a comb out of her purse and stroked her hair back into shape. It was piled sort of high on her head, like Tippi Hedren's hair in *The Birds*. When she was finished, she adjusted the lapels of her jacket and headed farther down the sidewalk. I watched her cross the street in the direction of the Hilton Hotel. I removed my disguise. Rather than directly follow her, I started the engine and pulled onto 14th and drove to the hotel. I pulled up at the end of the cab line. There were five cabs ahead of me. I glanced in my rear-view mirror and saw Mrs. Bombalini walking toward the Hilton.

She passed my cab, adjusting the collar on her shirt. She was beautiful. But because she was the wife of a client of mine, so to speak, I kept my eyes above her collar. I couldn't be held responsible for my peripheral vision though. It was going haywire.

The cab line moved forward every few minutes. I didn't turn on the AM radio or read my paperback. I just sat there staring at the front door of the Hilton. Francois had escorted her inside, so I thought about getting out and walking up to him and asking if he might give me the lowdown on the blonde who had entered the hotel. But I didn't do it. I could have done it. I could have followed her inside. I could have hoofed it a bit. I could have done a lot of things to earn my three bills. But instead, I just sat there waiting for Mrs. Bombalini to come back out.

After I agreed to do this job for Tony, I had started dreading it, as well as regretting it, and in some ways fearing it. But I hadn't expected to feel the emotion I was feeling right then. It reminded me of The Big Breakup between me and Mary Margaret Flaherty.

I was fairly young when we broke up, but I wasn't a kid. I'd been through the army, had spent two years in college, and thought I knew my own mind. That's one of the seven warning signs of youth. I thought I was in love with her. But I guess not marrying a guy who was destined to be broke all his life was all she was thinking about, i.e., why starve when you can eat? I suppose there's something to be said for nutrition, but as an English major I was viewing things from a romantic angle—specifically European Romanticism from 1789 through 1815.

I was second in the cab line when Mrs. Bombalini came walking out of the Hilton. I quickly put on my girl-glasses as a kind of instinctive move, as if I didn't want her to recognize me—now or ever. She walked past my cab bearing an anguished frown. I didn't know how to read that. I'm good at interpreting body language, but I don't speak woman.

I pulled out of the cab line and drove over to 15th and watched as Mrs. Bombalini walked across the parking lot, got into her car, and backed out of the slot. She pulled onto 14th and maneuvered her way toward Broadway, where she headed south. I followed. We were heading in the same direction I had driven when Tony and I had first gotten together to discuss this subterfuge. Up until then I had always rather liked the word "subterfuge," but now it left a bad taste in my mouth. Another one of my favorite words is "derelict." I don't know why I even brought that up.

Mrs. Bombalini turned left onto Speer Boulevard and headed east. I stayed behind her, changing lanes and keeping her Mercedes in sight. Speer turned into 1st Avenue. We rolled past the Denver Country Club and drove all the way to Cherry Creek Shopping Center. But she didn't go to the shopping center. She turned left into an area known as Cherry Creek North. Like Larimer Square, it had been developed over the years into a conglomeration of trendy boutiques.

I got caught at the red light where she had turned, but it bothered me only a little bit. I was sort of hoping that she would lose me. I imagined myself telling this to Tony. "She lost me at a red light." It would sound plausible. If Tony had known me better, it would have sounded inevitable. But when I made it around the corner I saw Mrs. Bombalini getting out of her Mercedes, parked at the curb in front of a bar called The Cherry Pit. She walked quickly into the bar like a woman who needed to walk quickly into a bar. That made me feel bad.

I drove up to the next block, parked at the curb, and sat for a minute. I decided to hoof it a bit. If she was meeting someone at the bar, I might as well see who it was. I wanted to give myself the impression that I was earning my pay.

I got out of my cab and walked back down the block. I had never been in The Cherry Pit before but from the outside it looked like a nice place. It was only a block away from Biloxi's where all this had started—sort of. It looked like the kind of place where a well-to-do housewife might go with her girlfriends for a quick snort after a shopping binge.

I reached for the doorknob but the door suddenly swung open and Mrs. Bombalini came out fast. We almost collided. "Pardon me," she said, barely glancing at me. I held the door open and let her go by. I went inside, then turned around and looked through a diamond-shaped window on the door. Mrs. Bombalini climbed into her Mercedes and drove away.

I gave the bar a quick glance. There were a few women seated at tables, their calves being massaged by shopping bags from Saks Fifth Avenue. The only man was the bartender who was wiping down the counter. I left the place fast and hurried up the street and got into my cab. Mrs. Bombalini had lost me.

For some reason I didn't mind the idea of lying to Tony about his wife losing me, but the idea of telling the truth made feel like a bumbling idiot. I began to panic. I drove up the street. I couldn't see the Mercedes anywhere. I began to get the feeling that I was going to be doing this again tomorrow, and gratis to boot. I wouldn't feel right charging Tony another three bills for a job I had bollixed. As a taxi driver my rule of thumb is to never gouge anybody for more than five dollars. I was way out of my league.

I continued driving north toward 6th Avenue, praying for a miracle. That has never worked.

Then I got a brainstorm. I decided to go back to the Bombalini house and wait to see if she came home. She had only a few minutes lead-time on me. I headed east on 6th, pushing it and keeping an eye out for cops.

It worked. I was already parked in her neighborhood when the Mercedes came down the block and turned into the driveway. I was wearing the girl-glasses again. I watched through my rear-view mirror as Mrs. Bombalini got out of her car and crossed the lawn to the front door.

I glanced down at my wristwatch. It was one o'clock. This was the fastest three bills I had ever made. Also the hardest. The job wasn't finished though. I still had to cross one tee and dot one eye. I had to get to a phone and make a call to Tony. But I had four hours to wait until I could do it. It would be the longest four hours of my life, not counting my army physical.

CHAPTER 14

While dawdling back toward downtown, I started thinking about whether or not to follow Sheila's advice and take care of the glasses business before she zapped me with another "Mm hmmm." I decided to capitulate. I figured four hours would give me enough time to get it done. I've succumbed to despair in less time than that.

There was a little optometrist shop on south Broadway tucked in between a pizza joint and what amounted to a head shop where you could buy glow-in-the-dark posters, bongs, and whatever else the hippies began marketing after they went commercial in the '70s. I had driven by there many times in my cab, and occasionally picked up Baby Boomers who smelled like patchouli. I also visited the pizza shop, a family-owned business where the pizzas were hand crafted—none of this fast-food mass-produced garbage that you get in eateries, which shall remain nameless because I also service them in my cab. But I had never visited the optometrist shop. The entrance had a 1930s look that I liked—art deco molded-tin awning over the doorway, and Bakelite tiles on the foyer walls. It looked like the kind of business that would be owned by an elderly optometrist who had serviced families for generations and personally ground lenses in his back room. I liked the look of the shop, but I drove right past it on my way to Sight City!!! where you could buy Two Pair for the Price of One!!! according to the billboards plastered all over Denver blocking every decent view of the Rocky Mountains.

There was a SightCity!!! in the shopping center across the street from the McDonald's where all of this had actually begun, and that's where I parked my cab. I removed Sheila's girl-glasses and hid them on the seat by my briefcase so the clerks in SightCity!!! wouldn't see them and start thinking I was "up to something."

When I got out and started walking toward the glass doors of Sight City!!! I began to feel furtive, as if I was entering a head shop. After all, why would anybody enter a head shop? To buy a velvet Elvis? Give me a break. But having never entered any sort of glasses store before I felt foolish, the way everybody feels foolish the first time they do anything, and I haven't really had all that much experience doing anything.

It was like a church in there. Or a mortuary. The floor was carpeted. The room was silent. A few other customers were trying on frames from rotating display racks. I walked past them the way I walk past bras at K-Mart—I kept my eyes fixed on a clerk standing behind a counter at the rear of the shop. She was wearing a white smock. She wasn't wearing glasses. That struck me as rather unprofessional.

"May I help you?" she said.

She was young. She was pretty. I doubted if I would ever learn her favorite color. "I failed my DOT test," I said. She frowned at me as women often do. I'll admit it. I was rattled. I was there to confess the shortcomings of my eyeballs.

After I confessed, she told me I would have to take an eye exam, then she gave me a dazzling smile and said it would take a little while to set it up. In the meantime I was welcome to examine their wide array of frames.

"Two for the price of one, it's the way that this thing is, right?" I managed to choke out like I had just gotten off the boat from Dublin.

"That is correct, sir. We also have a special on disposable contact lenses." But I was so relieved to learn I wasn't in for a rip job that I barely heard her. I mumbled no thanks and turned away and began examining a rack filled with white frames.

"The men's frames are in the far corner, sir," she said as she headed toward the back room.

I felt like I had been caught gawking at bras—but I guess we've all been there. I hurried to the far corner and tried to make myself as unobtrusive as possible while I browsed the masculine frames.

Well. Who did I want to look like for the rest of my life? Buddy Holly? John Lennon? I sneaked a glance at the other customers trying on frames and staring at themselves in mirrors. I finally made The Big Move. I reached out and plucked a pair of wire rimmed frames and quickly put them on without poking myself in the eye too badly. As I stood staring at my face in the mirror I felt like a raving egotist. It was a familiar feeling. I turned my head this way and that, and finally decided I didn't look at all like John Lennon.

I tried on another pair of frames plucked at random, on the theory that randomness had more to do with my life than volition. They were thick black frames. I looked like Mel Cooley. I took them off and tried on a different pair. After awhile my shyness faded. I began trying on every type of frame they had. I got to like it. I suddenly became Mister Frames. I was ready to run into the street and drag strangers into the store shouting, "It's easy! Don't be afraid!" It was like the first time I drank a beer.

I finally settled on a fairly conservative pair of frames, part wire, part brown plastic. I decided these would work, although I do have to admit I was attracted to the Mel Cooley persona. He was Alan Brady's producer, you know.

To make a long story short, I walked out of the store a new man. The world was a carousel of color. That's when I realized I was parked in a handicapped zone. My heart thudded. I ran to my ticket magnet and hopped in, keeping an eye out for cops. Somehow I had a feeling that my prescription for nearsightedness wouldn't impress John Law, although an expensive shyster might get me off with a warning.

On the way back toward midtown I kept looking at my face in the rear-view mirror. The glasses were like a brand new couch in a living room filled with junk. I wondered what other changes I might make to improve the overall effect. I had grown a beard in college because I was a liberal arts major and wanted to distinguish myself from people who were planning real careers. But I shaved it off in Pittsburgh after street people began hitting me up for spare change, thinking I was their spiritual brother. I noticed that they never seemed to bother truck drivers or, ironically, cab drivers. I was no longer as skinny as Olive Oyl by then. I still hadn't touched a base-ball, but they did make me use a pugil stick one time in basic training. And I was making fairly good progress on the gut I had sown as a Boy Scout at Wa-Ni-Ta-Ka. Without my beard, I sort of looked like a redneck even though I was trying to become a writer, except one who actually made money as opposed to the other kind.

I didn't see much potential for improvement on my face that day. My eyes did keep drifting up to the shag on top of my head. I couldn't help but think that a professional haircut might offset my new glasses in the way that muted tones act as counterpoints to explosions of color in a Jackson Pollock painting.

Then I began thinking about Tony.

I began thinking I could drive to east Denver and wait for Uncle Gino to leave the barbershop, then I could walk right in and make my report face-to-face before five o'clock—and get that free haircut. I have never liked to engage in important conversations over the phone anyway.

By "important" I mean such things as apologies, requests for forgive-ness, beseeching in general, and the occasional passing along of bad news, such as telling someone I accidentally did it again, whatever it was. I prefer to say these things face-to-face because I consider the phone to be a cow-ardly instrument. In fact, I know it's a cowardly instrument because I have used it for especially embarrassing apologies for deeds so obnoxious that the idea of speaking to my victims face-to-face sent me tumbling into an abyss of such bleak ... well, let's drop it.

I simply felt it would be better to talk about these things with Tony in person. I started to head for east Denver, but then it occurred to me that I could just as easily drop off my cab at Rocky and go home and make the phone call to Tony from the womb of my apartment. What the hell. I had my three hundred bucks, and anyway, I never intended to see Tony again. Just as with Mary Margaret Flaherty, I would make a clean break.

I was so pleased with this new plan that I pounded my fist on the seat with excitement and broke Sheila's black-rimmed girl-glasses. I slowly raised my fist and looked for blood. Maybe she would feel sorry for me. But—no blood. One lens was shattered and an ear thing was broken off. What do they call those long deals that hook over your ears? Prows?

I felt awful. Then I thought maybe I could avoid Sheila for the rest of my life. I examined that ploy from every angle, and decided to get real. It wasn't until I arrived at the motor that it occurred to me to tell the truth. I had never gone that route before.

I looked at myself in the rear-view mirror and adjusted my new glasses tightly before I got out of the cab. I had never known Sheila to punch anybody out, at least not anybody wearing glasses. I gathered up my keys, tripsheet, briefcase, and ex-girl-glasses, and walked into the on-call room. I went up to the cage. Rollo was eating a donut. He stopped in mid-bite and stared at me. He set the donut down and leaned back in his chair, clasped his hands over his belly, and studied my new "look."

"You weren't wearing those glasses when you signed in this morning," he said. "Did your eyes go bad during your shift?"

This was a delicate moment. I knew where the bastard was headed. It was exactly where I would go if I ever "got the goods" on him—to Hogan's office.

"Yes," I said.

That pulled him up short.

Then Sheila walked into the on-call room and put an end to this subtle battle of the intellects.

"Looking good, Murph my man," she piped. "I'm proud of you."

Rollo surrendered and picked up his donut. Sheila held out her hand. I knew what she wanted. I also knew where she could get two for the price of one, on my nickel.

I held up the broken glasses and said, "I'm sorry. I sat on them." That was as close to the truth as I was willing to go.

She frowned a deep frown, then shook her head. "Don't mean nothing. These are just two-dollar reading glasses I bought at K-Mart."

The world became a carousel again. I pulled three dollars from my shirt pocket and held them out to her. She took all three.

"Quitting early?" she said.

"I had a good day," I replied.

Then Rollo broke in. "Your trip-sheet isn't filled out," he said with a victorious smile. "It looks to me like you didn't have any fares today."

I reached for the sheet but he pulled it away from my grasp. "I had one personal," I said.

Rollo reluctantly handed the sheet back. I took a moment to scribble in some info on a single trip for the day. One fare, one long ride around the city. A classic scenic route. This was not an unusual entry. When you snagged a trip to Vail or Aspen, you almost never showed more than two fares entered for the entire day—like my ride to Vail that turned into The Trip From Hell. Remind me to tell you that story sometime.

I signed out. It was getting toward three o'clock. I climbed into my heap, whispered, "Jaysus," and headed home. For a change of pace I made a quick stop at a Burger King and bought a Whopper and a chocolate shake. I didn't feel like cooking that night or doing the dish. When I got home, my crow's nest never looked so good to me.

The building I live in had been a private home back in the nineteenth century, but had been turned into apartments after Denver went broke. My apartment was way above the fray of the city, so I felt like a pirate climbing up to a crow's nest whenever I made the long trip up the three-story fire escape. I felt safe up there. The apartment could also be accessed by a staircase, which wound down through the interior of the building itself, but I almost never entered by the front door—my method of avoiding my neighbors, which I am good at.

I set my briefcase on the kitchen table and took out the other pair of glasses for the price of one. I carried them into my bedroom and put them into a dresser drawer for safekeeping, right next to an overdue library book.

I returned to the living room and took off the glasses I was wearing and tucked them into the carrying pouch that I would eventually lose. I knew I would lose it. I knew I would put the glasses safely into the pouch for a week, and then stop kidding myself. The pouch would disappear. The lenses would become a bit scratched up. I knew this without ever having owned glasses before, But I have owned other things.

I ate my burger and drank my shake, then went into the living room and began lethargically surfing the tube, thinking about the call I would have to make at a quarter after five. I wished I had told Tony ten after five. Time was slowing to a crawl. I thought about digging through my steamer trunk and finding a manuscript to work on, but I was afraid this would bring time to a complete halt and the universe would collapse.

I finally made a desperation move. I pulled out my Rubik's Cube. This killed forty-five minutes. Afterward I had to fight off the urge to dismantle the cube to see what made it work. I had been fighting that battle for eighteen years. It was a battle I knew I would lose someday, similar to the battle to make all the cube's colors match up. I've never done it. I once saw a twelve-year-old boy on TV solve the mystery of the cube in less than a minute. But I figured it was just a trick—he probably already knew how to do it. To me, knowing how to do something is like cheating.

That's why I never studied in grade school. Studying made passing tests too easy. Anybody can pass a test if he studies. But I wanted to explore the furthest limit of my *inh'rnt* knowledge. Apparently my limit is C minus.

CHAPTER 15

At a quarter after five I dialed Tony's phone number. I heard the receiver rattle at the other end.

"Gino's Barbershop. Tony speaking."

"Tony," I said. "This is Murph. Can you talk?"

"Yes, Gino's not here."

I talked. I told him everything that had happened from the moment Angelina left the house. He didn't say a word during my narrative, didn't ask any questions, didn't make any comments. Every now and then I would hear a shuffling at the other end of the line, the kind of sound you hear when someone's ear gets tired. I even told Tony the part where Angelina lost me at The Cherry Pit, but for some reason I didn't feel like a bumbling idiot. I felt like a normal human being, which doesn't speak well for mankind.

The narrative ended when Angelina stepped inside the Bombalini house and closed the door. There was a silence at the other end of the line. I decided to put an end to the silence by talking. I didn't know how else to do it.

"Will you need me again tomorrow?" I said, even though I had intended not to bring that subject up. It could lead to more work, and I instinctively avoid anything that leads anywhere.

"I won't need you again tomorrow, Murph, you've done enough." He thanked me for the job I had done and said he wouldn't be needing my services any further. He then told me he had to get home. I said goodbye. He hung up.

I stared at the receiver in my hand, then slowly set it on the cradle. I reached up and touched the bulge in my shirt pocket where the folded bills had been all afternoon, riding close to my heart where all money rides. I had earned my pay. The job was done. Over. Completed. Concluded. Finished. I thought about pulling out my thesaurus, but I got the message: I was quits with the Bombalini family.

I sat back in my chair and pulled the bulge out of my pocket and stared at it. Thirty sawbucks. New and clean and crisp. The kind of money you get from banks and not from cab drivers. What a racket banking is. People pay other people to hold onto their money. I wonder how you start a bank.

But here's the funny part. As new and crisp and clean as the money in my hand was, it felt dirty. I had a bad taste in my mouth and a clammy feeling in my gut. I had earned more money than I had ever earned in two hours in my life, and everything about it felt wrong. I got up and crossed the living room and reached for my *Finnegans Wake,* but then I stopped. Instead, I picked up my paperback copy of *Lolita* and stuffed the bills inside it and set it back on the shelf. This may have been Freudian, but it wasn't a slip. Three copies of *Lolita* already had been stolen from my bookshelf, but that was back in the days before I wised up and quit inviting my friends over. The notion that a burglar might sneak into my apartment and steal a Nabokov novel was far-fetched, but what's that got to do with my life? At any rate, I no longer wanted anything to do with the money.

This was not a good attitude because my rent was coming due and I had missed two days of work this week. Who invented "rent?" Probably Moog, the bastard.

I sat back down and stared at the blank screen of my TV. I stared at it so long that it occurred to me I had never really looked at a TV that wasn't on. I noticed that the screen was kind of gray/green. I then wondered why the cathode-ray tube lasted so long when every goddamn light bulb in my apartment burned out after six weeks.

I had gone through a lot of used TVs since I fled Wichita. My first one cost forty dollars. I had bought it at a Salvation Army store the same day I blew into Atlanta. It lasted three years. It gave up its ghosts in Pittsburgh. I've owned all kinds of TVs, large and small, color and black and white. I have never been without a TV. I began to wonder if I could make some money writing a magazine article about "TVs I Have Known And Loved." My thoughts always turn to money when I'm broke. The fact that I wasn't really broke told me something I didn't want to hear: if I didn't use the three bills to pay my rent, I was going to have to come up with another way to make back the money I had not earned this week.

There was something wrong with the Bombalini money. The thought of spending it on anything at all gave me a sour feeling. What was Tony going to do with the information I had given him? I didn't want to think about it. I turned on the TV. It didn't help. I kept thinking.

I decided I didn't want to use that three hundred to help pay my rent for next month. I wanted to pay my rent with money that didn't feel wrong. But I didn't have that kind of money right then.

When an asphalt warrior finds himself backed into a financial corner, he has a limited number of options. Since the maximum number of hours he can legally drive during a given shift is twelve, he is forced to drive faster, not smarter. He has to forego the joe and the Twinkie and stay away from the hotels and take every feasible call that comes over the radio. He has to hump the bells. He has to keep a quick eye out for pedestrians hailing rides from the sidewalk. He has to keep moving because speed is money in this game.

However, there was one other option that I resisted thinking about. I began surfing the channels, looking for Mary Ann, but the castaways were nowhere to be seen. This was odd when you considered how many reruns existed on ninety cable channels running 24/7. But I recognized it. It was a sign from God. Okay, let's cut to the chase. I'm talking Catholic guilt.

The three hundred bucks didn't merely seem like a lot of money to a man who had never earned that much dough in a single day in his life, it seemed like an outrageous rip job. I had been paid three hundred a month in the army. If my Maw found out I had earned three hundred dollars in two hours she would have marched me straight down to Blessed Virgin Catholic Church and made me put half of it into the Poor Box. And if she found out how I had earned it she would have herded me into a confessional and held onto my left ear while I came clean with Monsignor O'Leary.

Jaysus.

Right at that moment I wished I was sitting behind the steering wheel of 127 and just driving, driving, driving. This was how I usually dealt with guilt: staying on the move and trying not to think. When I was a kid I did it on a bicycle. I once played hooky from church when I was eleven. This was after "The Wa-Ni-Ta-Ka Incident," when I was totally corrupted for life.

Back then my Maw always attended six A.M. mass, a High Mass, the Latin Mass reserved for the old pros. But instead of going to my usual noon mass that Sunday in Wichita, I rode my bicycle to a penny arcade and blew my weekly allowance on pinball. After I walked out of the joint I couldn't believe what I had done. A banshee followed me all the way home. When I got into the house my Maw innocently asked me what the good father's sermon had been about, and I ran into the bathroom and locked the door. She knocked on the door and asked me what was wrong. I told her I was sick. For the first time in my life I wasn't lying. I was vomiting.

End of story.

I switched off the TV and stared at the blank screen until I finally admitted to myself that there was only one way out of this mess: The Dreaded Weekend Lease.

Rocky Cab offers a special arrangement for drivers who don't want to work a sane and sensible five-day week, or the daily lease that butters my own bread. For a discount you can lease a taxi for the weekend, beginning on Friday morning and ending on Sunday night. You have to pay $180.00 up front rather than $210.00 for the three days. But you have access to the cab twenty-four hours a day. The problem with the weekend lease is that you have to earn the one-eighty plus gas before you see a dime of profit. It takes nerves of steel. Weekends are a gamble. Businessmen don't make as many airport runs on Saturdays and Sundays. Fridays and Mondays are the big airport days in Denver. DIA is hopping.

The advantage is that you can make better money than on weekdays by working the busy hours, the bars closings, the theater and restaurant crowds. You can sign in over the radio, and sign out again whenever you want. You can drive when there are "shoes on the sidewalk," as we cabbies say, and tap into the most lucrative times of the day. You can crash in your pad during the lulls, the dead time, the wee small hours of the morning when the radio is quiet. But you can grab only a few winks before it's time to crawl out of the sack and hit the road running. The weekend lease is the most exacting and unforgiving test of an asphalt warrior's knowledge, competence, and endurance.

I call it "The Anvil."

I got out of my chair and walked into the kitchen. I needed a drink bad. Real bad. But as I pulled a brew from the fridge, I suddenly stopped. For the next three days I would be like a Spartan soldier going into battle stripped to a breechcloth and carrying nothing more than a double-edged sword, a will to win, and a bottle of No-Doz.

I placed the beer back on the rack.

I turned off the lights, went into the bedroom, kicked off my Keds, and started praying.

It's a funny thing about determination. It empties you of all emotion. You become focused. You become an automaton. I might as well admit that when I normally get up to go to work I vaguely hope that my Chevy will be stolen so I can go back to bed and wait for a friendly cop to activate my snooze alarm. But car thieves aren't as reliable as they used to be. My heap was in my parking lot when I stepped outside that Friday morning.

I drove to Rocky feeling empty of everything except the thought of the next three days. I might not see a dime of profit until noon Saturday, depending on how things went. It's a strange feeling going to work knowing that you won't be putting any money in your pocket that day. Of course, everybody does that during the first three months of each fiscal year. Rocky Cab has a lot in common with Uncle Sam.

I parked in the lot, then took a moment to examine my new glasses in my rear-view mirror. I couldn't help but notice my hair. It made me think of Tony. It made me think of the three hundred dollars tucked into my shirt pocket. I was going to use some of those spic-and-span bills to pay for my weekend lease. After all, the sense that they were dirty was merely an abstraction. I would pay them back, so to speak, after this was all over. But they were my only hope of paying for a long lease up front. "Hope" is another abstraction that I rarely take seriously.

I walked into the on-call room and saw Rollo sucking the vanilla filling from an éclair—his Friday delicacy. The smell of éclairs and big money is always in the air on Friday, the most lucrative day of the week for cab drivers. Shoes are on the sidewalk. The room is filled with early risers eager to get out on the road. Most of them are old pros. Only a few newbies mingle with the crowd waiting for taxis to come in from the night shift. There's a lot of ebullience and horseplay on Friday. I can't stand ebullience. But that morning I was focused.

I went up to the window of the cage, pulled my wad from my shirt pocket, and began peeling off bills. Rollo paused in mid-suck and watched my hands curiously.

"I want a weekend lease," I said. A hush fell over the room.

I heard my name whispered here and there, and a few I-don't-believe-its. I had a rep at Rocky. It had been more than ten years since I had worked hard.

Rollo leaned over and quietly whispered something into his intercom Then he took my money and counted it out. I waited while he gathered three trip-sheets together and made a few notes on his blotter. He seemed to be taking a little longer than usual to do the paperwork. Say what I will about Rollo's detestable personality, he's a good cage man. I suddenly got the feeling he was buying time.

Then Hogan walked in.

Everyone turned and looked at the supervisor. He was staring straight at me. He crossed the room and stopped in front of me.

"Morning, Murph," he said.

"Morning," I said.

"Nice glasses."

"Thanks."

He held out a hand. "Mind if take a look at them?" I glanced at Rollo. His face was obscenely angelic. I removed my glasses and handed them over.

Hogan turned the specs this way and that, then removed his own pop-bottles and peered through my lenses. He nodded and handed them back. "Just checking," he said with a smile.

As I say—I have a rep at Rocky.

CHAPTER 16

You know the drill. No need to go into too much detail. It was a Friday like all Fridays. People were fleeing their jobs for the weekend, heading for the airport or entering hotels, entering bars, catching movies and plays, seeking something that was missing from their lives on the weekdays, and generally scattering like ants all over the city. I played the Friday game. I played it long and I played it hard.

During the Friday evening rush hour I went home and slept. The interstates are jammed at the rush. The Mousetrap is packed with bodies going nowhere, like most mousetraps. The Tech Center is a parking lot. I made it back to my crow's nest by four and slept for three hours, then dove in for the Friday night foot traffic: the theatergoers, the late shoppers, the undrunk looking for the cure, and the Happy Hour executives leaving for the Unhappy Hour at home.

Business always begins easing off the streets between nine and midnight. That's when I planned to take my next break. My AM radio was shut off between seven and nine. My ears were locked onto the Rocky boom box. I humped the bells. I listened for runs from the blood bank, for hotels, and Union Station. I became one with the vocal chords of the dispatcher. The microphone was glued to the palm of my hand. I was hitting the button like a telegraph operator. Grabbing calls became a race between me and the old pros. The newbies were shut out. The air waves were frantic. And then at nine P.M. the radio went silent. I was parked at a curb near the intersection of Colfax and Broadway, positioned to head in any direction. But the radio remained silent. I finally pried the mike from my fist. I leaned back against the seat and took a deep breath.

I had one hundred and thirty dollars in my shirt pocket. I was still down ten for the gas, and my gauge was nearing empty. I had to make another twenty for the rest of the weekend gas, plus another fifty to cover the lease, plus whatever I could snatch to stuff into my *Finnegans* when all this was over. Numbers were spinning in front of my eyes like bluebirds in front of Sylvester's after Tweety dropped a bowling ball on his head. My grade school teachers would have been stunned, too. I couldn't think straight anymore. I was still down, still wasn't making any profit, but I had the bastard on the run. You know who I'm talking about—the bastard who drags you out of bed at dawn and says, "Cut bait or fish, chump, this is a working man's boat."

I drove back to my apartment with barely enough strength to whisper, "Jesus."

I crashed in my pad. My alarm was set for eleven-thirty P.M. I wanted to be back on the road before midnight. There was a time in Denver when the 3.2 bars closed at midnight, but the government decided that eighteen was too young to drink beer but not too young to die for love and glory. I had mixed feelings about that and still do. I don't know how I would have made it through the army without getting swacked every payday, and all the days in between.

I fell into an uneasy sleep. I was driving down a long tunnel made of asphalt. Stop signs were hanging from the ceiling. I couldn't find my glasses. I was careening toward the dark at the end of the tunnel. I looked into the rear-view mirror and saw Tony weeping in the backseat. "... *myyy ba-bee does the hanky-panky ...*"

I reached out and slapped the radio off and sat up rubbing the asphalt out of my eyes. The clock said 11:30. It felt like tomorrow but I was still stuck in yesterday. I staggered into the kitchen, made a cheese sandwich, grabbed my briefcase and a Coke, and headed out the door.

I signed in over the radio. The dispatcher wished me a good morning. The Word was out: Murph is walking with the zombies. Luck was on my side. A Happy Hour drunk had been thrown out of his house five minutes away from my apartment and he wanted to go to a motel on south Broadway.

As soon as I dropped him off at the Bide-A-Wee, I caught two couples coming out of a bar that wanted to catch a midnight flick at the Mayan Theater up near 1st and Broadway—Rocky Horror Picture Show. The '70s would never die. This took me in the direction of midtown. As I was letting them out, another couple approached from the theater and said they had called Yellow Cab an hour earlier but the taxi hadn't shown up. I dragged them into my backseat and stomped on the accelerator. There's only two kinds of cabbies working the mean streets of Denver on a Friday night: the quick and the quicker.

Saturday arrived. I'm talking twelve midnight. For the next two hours the drunks would be filtering out of the bars. Two A.M. signaled "the little rush hour" when the bars closed and the drunks had nowhere to go but home. I had to make an attitude adjustment. Most of my driving in the past few years had been day shifts. You rarely got drunks while pulling days. Drunks are one of the reasons I don't like to do nights. Drunks like to talk, and talking to drunks is worse than talking to sober people. Talking to sober people is the drawback of days.

The two A.M. bar bells can be a real freak show. You get the laughers, the lovers, the weepers, the philosophers, the politicos, the poets, and the tough guys. It's a ship of fools, a mixed crew, but they all have one thing in common: they over-tip.

That's the lure of driving nights, and the reason so many cabbies prefer it. It's like the Dutchman's Lost Gold Mine to a lot of old pros. You head out into the wasteland on your tin burro and fight the heat, the rattlesnakes, the gully washers, and the loneliness, but you come back to civilization with bags of gold.

Fool's gold, in my opinion. But I admire the old pros who can handle it on a regular basis. Not envy, just admire. When I'm looking for the treasure of the Sierra Madre, I turn on my TV.

But I did all right between midnight and last call. I didn't have any problems with the drunks. They were an affable lot. To be honest, Saturday night is the main event when it comes to picking up fares at bars. The rummies have had two nights to work themselves into a frenzy before Sunday morning coming down. I did get one philosopher who said he was convinced that within the next twenty years the states of New Mexico, Arizona, and California would be annexed to Mexico, while Oregon, Washington, Idaho, and Alaska would become provinces of Canada. I agreed with him wholeheartedly. He gave me twenty bucks on a fourteen-dollar fare.

By two thirty I had made my nut and covered the gas for the next two days. Everything from here on out would be clear profit. If I kept up the same pace as Friday I would be way ahead of the game. But I didn't kid myself. My years on the asphalt had taught me that you never get ahead in this game. You tread water, you keep your head afloat, but the *Queen Mary* never arrives with a lounge chair reserved for you on the A Deck. Ergo, you only bust your ass in a financial emergency. You take your meager profits and go home because there's always tomorrow. That's the good news and the bad news. There's always tomorrow.

I got back to my crow's nest at three A.M., no longer worried about making up for the two days I had lost during the week. My biggest worry had been earning back the one-eighty lease payment, even though there was no rational reason to worry. A cabbie might come home broke, but he almost always earns back the lease. It's virtually a law of physics. However, personal profit is relegated to the science of astrology—nobody is certain if it's for real, but a lot of crackpots seem to think so.

I collapsed into bed feeling the way I had felt on a number of occasions in my life, which primarily had involved quitting, or at least not doing something any longer. I felt the way I had felt when I graduated from high school, when I received my army discharge, when I dropped out of college, when I walked off every job I ever walked off or got fired from: I felt both great and free. That night I dreamed I was sitting in my cab sleeping. The cab seemed to be stopped in a major intersection. Cops and other people kept pounding on my windows, but I just kept snoozing. At least ... I think it was a dream.

I woke up in my apartment at eleven thirty on Saturday morning, well rested and ready to go out and start scooping gold out of the asphalt river that meanders out of Denver and into every city in America. Each dime I took in would belong to me from here to Sunday night. I had survived the crucible of The Anvil and was in the same position that apprentice salesmen are often told they're in—the amount of money you earn is entirely up to you. Hey, I want to earn five grand a day. "Okay, boy, here's your sample case—now get out there and sell!"

That's one adult job I've never held. Salesman. Dyna-Plex had salesmen on their staff. I don't know what they sold. But whenever I interviewed salesmen for "the brochure" they always said things like, "You don't sell the steak, you sell the sizzle," and "First you sell yourself, then you sell the product." I used to write these things down on my yellow pad next to "more bang for your buck" and "reinvent the wheel." Then I would go smoke a cigarette.

Before I left to drive that Saturday, I opened my *Finnegans Wake* and did some accounting. I removed three hundred dollars and stuffed it into *Lolita*. Payback time. The three hundred felt dirty again. It made me think of Tony. I shut that off and left the apartment, went downstairs and climbed into 127. I signed in over the radio, then drove to a 7-11 on Capitol Hill to pick up some joe and a Twinkie.

I parked in the lot and went inside. Katy was on the job behind the counter that day. Katy was a former stripper who once told me she took the job working at 7-11 because she was tired of dealing with weird people. Note that her 7-11 was located in the heart of Capitol Hill, adjacent to a #15 bus stop. The 15 bus is a traveling circus. It runs along Colfax Avenue. Colfax is Denver's Tenderloin, or Bowery, or Bellevue, pick your favorite nightmare. You get the picture. And if you don't—steer clear of Colfax.

There was a line of street freaks waiting at the counter, which was not unusual, so I didn't have time for in-depth repartee with Katy. I didn't even glance at the lottery tickets under the glass display case. She asked me why I was working on a Saturday. I told her it had something to do with the rent. She winked at me. That made my day. Did I mention she was an ex-stripper?

I went outside and got into my cab and sat for a minute sipping at my joe and eyeing my Twinkie. Then a pedestrian ambushed me.

He opened my right rear door and asked if I could take him to the Denver Police Department. I looked around at him. He was about twenty years old. He was wearing a black overcoat. His hair was punk long, unkempt and greasy. I didn't like his looks but I liked his destination.

"Hop in," I said.

A fare is a fare, but I wasn't thrilled because twenty-year-old males don't tip. For reasons that I'll never understand, society has never explained tipping to young males. I myself didn't learn about it until I started going to bars that sold whiskey. On the other hand, all women know about tipping. I would rather not speculate as to why. Waitresses are the best tippers. They often over-tip. Waitresses and cabbies have a lot of things in common, and savvy is one of them.

As soon as the kid settled onto the backseat he said, "I'm a poet."

I turned on the meter fast. "DPD huh?" I said, trying to get him off the subject.

"That's right," he said. "I have a meeting with my parole officer."

Before I had a chance to ask what he had gotten busted for, he said, "Would you like to hear one of my poems?"

I started to panic. In my line of work the customer is always right, as long as he tips according to Hoyle. But I knew this young male wasn't even in the game. Instead of replying, I drove onto Colfax headed west, my head turning this way and that scanning the traffic. I was trying to appear conscientious and distracted.

"I've only written two lines so far," he continued, oblivious of my ruse.

I calmed down. How bad could two lines be? That was a rhetorical question. Two lines could start World War III in the right venue

I glanced back at the kid. He looked like every bohemian I had known since the '60s. I realized now that his hair wasn't punk long, it was poet long. Two lines, I told myself. You survived the army, you can survive a poem. "Lay it on me, daddy."

His face lit up. He cleared his throat and raised his chin: "A renegade priest, from a town in the east ..."

He stopped and cleared his throat. "That's as far as I've gotten."

I nodded. "It rhymes, but I won't hold that against you. I like it."

He grinned big. Then frowned. "I can't think of what I should write next."

The hairs on the back of my neck started to prickle. He kept talking. "I've showed it to a lot of people, but nobody seems to know where the poem should go. So ..." again he cleared his throat, "... I thought maybe I should ask a cab driver, since they know all about life and stuff."

I glanced in the rear-view mirror, then looked at the meter. Eight more blocks and we would be at DPD. I took a deep breath, smiled affably, and glanced back.

"You're tactic is correct even if your strategy is a bust," I said. "Cab drivers know a lot, but nobody can tell a poet where to go with his poems," except me. But he was my fare, my bread-and-butter, my lifeline to this month's rent. "You have to find that inside yourself, pal. But I'll tell you this much. Already I'm wondering about that town in the east. Why did he leave the place? And what makes the priest a renegade? You have a lot to work with there."

Rod McKuen leaned forward. I could smell his breath. It smelled like Sen-Sen.

"Do you really think it's good?"

"What is good?" I said, buying time. We were almost at police head-quarters. "Good is a finished poem, if it's going to be good at all. But I think you've got the makings of a small epic there, or at least a country song. I say give it some more thought. People are gonna want to know why that priest left town, and where he went afterwards. And depending on the direction the poem takes, they're gonna want to know how he died in the end."

"Do you think I should kill him off?" he said, as bright-eyed and eager as I used to look when I took creative writing at UCD. "Definitely," I replied, pulling up at the curb. "Put the poor guy out of his misery. But make sure his death is redeeming."

The kid frowned as he fumbled in his coat pocket for some money. "How do I do that?" he said.

The red flag was up. The ride was over. I shrugged. "Scour your heart," I said. "That's where the seeds of death reside."

The kid handed me five dollars on a three-forty fare and told me to keep the change. This made me feel bad. I watched as he trundled across the vast concrete apron fronting DPD. I pegged him as a pot bust. Generally I avoid poets. A cab driver is a sitting duck though, so you never know what's going to climb into your backseat. But I hardly ever encounter poets. They rarely get up in the daytime, which is their only saving grace.

CHAPTER 17

I began drifting toward the hotels and listening to the dispatcher. But I kept thinking about that poem. Why a renegade? Why a priest? I turned on the AM radio. *"...myyy ba-bee does the hanky-panky ..."* and switched it off. Why a renegade? Why a priest? The kid's lines had gotten under my skin. Just to get even I thought of driving back to DPD and telling the parole officer that the poet had left a lid of Maui Wowie on my backseat. But I decided to try and find a short line at a hotel instead. Maybe I could catch a rich man going to DIA, or a rich woman looking for love in all the wrong taxis.

I finally pulled into line at the Brown Palace. Three cabs ahead of me. Not too bad. I shut everything down and picked up my paperback. I read for half an hour. The three cabs picked up passengers, and I eventually cruised up to the first spot in line and shut off my engine, feeling the tingle of impending fares. Being first in a cab line is like being first in any line, a checkout line, an unemployment line, a theater line. It's showtime. I set my book aside. It's impossible to concentrate when fifty dollars might come walking out of a hotel. You watch the front door like a crouching cat watching an old lady carrying a tin of tuna toward an electric can opener.

Then a pedestrian ambushed me. He tapped on my window.

I almost shouted, *There is no justice in this world! Walking should be outlawed! My fifty dollars! My precious!*

I rolled the window down and said, "Yes?"—meaning, go away.

The man leaned closer and said, "Listen, I need you to do something for me." He seemed rattled. He pointed toward 18th Street and said, "There's this old fellow on crutches standing in the doorway of a building three blocks from here. He's a cripple. He can't get around by himself. I'll pay you ten dollars if you'll go pick him up. He wants to go to the Tip-Top Inn on Fifteenth Street." As he spoke, the man began digging quickly through his billfold, one of the most pleasant sights on earth.

I calmed down and pretended not to keep glancing at his money every tenth of a second.

The man held out a sawbuck and said, "He told me he has been trying to flag down taxis, but none of them will stop for him."

I grew ashamed of my asphalt brethren. Of course cab drivers are not required by regulations to stop for pedestrians waving frantically from a curb, but when you toss crutches into the picture, give me an asphalt break.

I pulled away from the curb and watched in the mirror as another cab pulled into my place in line. I felt like I had been robbed of fifty dollars. A cab driver's sense of entitlement is an awesome thing to behold.

I found the address. I then realized why nobody had stopped for him. He was leaning against a wall inside a recessed entrance to an old hotel built of red sandstone. Even I had trouble spotting him. I forgave my asphalt brethren. That was a first for me.

The man waved frantically. I pulled over to the curb and hopped out. He was coatless, leaning on his crutches, wearing a shoe on one foot and a slipper on the other. He looked to be in his sixties. Hatless. Hair stringy, and wispy where it wasn't balding, his ragged shirt half-buttoned, his belly exposed. I was astonished by his wretched appearance and keep in mind that one of my favorite movies is *Barfly*.

I hurried around and opened the rear door and escorted him to the curb. "I have a hard time sitting down," he said. "You'll have to take it easy. My hip is broken."

I held the crutches while he eased himself into the cab. He knew how to do it. He probably spent all his time easing onto seats. His slipper fell off and landed in the gutter where a thin stream of water was flowing. I grabbed it out of the water, then saw the man's foot. It was a mass of bleeding sores. Where did this guy come from? Did he escape from a mental institution? I eased the slipper back onto his foot, then noted that he was having trouble twisting around to get settled on the seat. I took his leg by the ankle and tried to maneuver it into the cab. He began screaming. It was a woman's scream. "My hip! My hip!"

I freaked. I have no business touching carburetors, much less human beings.

He lay down on the backseat. I gently closed the door and hurried around to the driver's side. The Tip-Top was only six blocks away and I wanted to get this horror show over with as quickly as possible.

I started the engine, pulled into traffic, and inhaled an odor so vile that my lungs almost collapsed. It came from the man in the backseat, a smell unlike anything I had ever encountered in my entire life. I was on the verge of vomiting. I rolled down my window and stuck my head out and inhaled the breeze created by the motion of the taxi. I kept my head outside all the way to the Tip-Top.

As soon as I parked at the curb I threw the door open, dove out, and gulped fresh air.

I finally went around to the passenger side and opened the door. The man seemed to know how to get out on his own. He grabbed the door and hauled himself to a standing position. "Thank you, thank you," he said. I reached into the backseat and retrieved his crutches. "Do you need help getting into the bar?"

"No," the man said. "If you can just help me to the wall, I'll be all right."

Surreptitiously holding my breath, I took hold of the man's arm and escorted him to the wall.

"Are you sure you don't need help getting inside?" I said, but the man shook his head no and said he would be okay. He leaned against the wall.

I walked to my cab, opened each door, and began rolling the windows all the way down. I shut the doors and got into the driver's seat and looked at the man up against the wall. I wondered how anybody could bring themselves to sit next to him in a bar. Who would help him home? Did he have any friends? Where did he live? The same questions I often asked of myself at two A.M. in Sweeney's.

I wondered if I should call the cops, or an ambulance. But I knew in my gut that I was looking at a survivor who was living in a world he had shaped through experience and knew how to handle. I decided not to intervene. I might upset the delicate balance of his fragile existence, which is my specialty.

When I got back to the Brown Palace there were three cabs ahead of me in line again. I parked at the end, closed my eyes and whispered the Cab Driver's Prayer: "It doesn't matter, it doesn't matter, it doesn't matter." Then I opened my paperback and tried to pick up the thread of the plot.

I'll admit it. Every once in awhile I'll read a book that has a plot. I was weaned from plots in college, but there comes a time when a man gets tired of reading detailed descriptions of the inner landscapes of characters whose pointless lives are ground to ash by their inability to move in any direction. I get enough of that on the interstate.

I couldn't keep my mind on the book though. I kept reading the same paragraph over and over. True, it was a sex scene, but I finally lowered the book and stared out the front window.

I kept thinking about the vow I had once taken. Not the vow never to take a physical empty-bladdered, but the vow never to get involved in a fare's personal life. I backtracked in my mind, trying to figure out how I had gotten involved with Tony. It was a short trip. It ended at McDonald's on Broadway and Alameda where he had offered me three hundred dollars to do something I vowed I would never do again. Money was the crux of the matter. Money is always the crux. But it still didn't explain why I was willing to break that vow. What have I ever really cared about money? I've always wanted to be rich, but I couldn't recall ever putting out any serious effort in that direction, unless you counted lottery tickets.

Nevertheless, I kept trying to figure out why money had made me do something I didn't want to do. Was there some mysterious connection between money and doing things? Then I started thinking: why a renegade, why a priest? It didn't have anything to do with the Bombalini business but it took my mind off it. And then, just as I was lifting the Coke to my lips, I got a call over the radio that made my hair stand on end.

"One twenty-seven, you've got a personal in east Denver," the dispatcher said. He gave me the address.

It was Tony Bombalini's house.

Even though I already knew the address and how to get there, I wrote it down on a piece of paper. I had been yelled at by the dispatcher once this year and I wasn't certain it wouldn't happen again in the next half hour. But more than that, I didn't want to get yelled at by Big Al. He was as close to a conscience as I had possessed since I left Wichita. The English professors call it personification—"attributing human qualities to an inanimate object." Close enough.

I pulled out of the cab line and made my way over to Colfax. I drove up Capitol Hill past the golden dome, past the spot where I had dropped off the troublemaker on Monday, and continued east. The dispatcher didn't tell me who had requested my services at the Bombalini household, and suddenly I wanted to know. I wanted to know bad.

Real bad.

I slowed as I approached the 7-11 where Katy worked. There were three public telephones on the wall outside. I pulled into the parking lot. I got out of my cab and examined them. The first phone appeared to have grape jelly smeared all over the receiver. The second phone looked intact, until I noticed the receiver cord missing. But the third phone was in working condition. I dropped two quarters into the slot and dialed the number of Gino's Barbershop. Even though I had called Gino's only one time, I had the number memorized. The nuns would have been stunned. But that's what comes from working with numbers in real life rather than sitting at a desk memorizing a textbook. I'm still convinced that school is a hoax.

The phone started ringing.

I was holding the receiver with my right arm cocked in the quick hang-up position. I had perfected the quick hang-up from years of calling people I didn't want to talk to. If Uncle Gino answered, my right arm would go into action.

The phone kept ringing.

My plan was to find out if Tony was at the shop that afternoon. If he was, it would indicate that his wife might have called Rocky Cab from the

Bombalini house. Or maybe even Gino. I wanted to know what I was driving into.

The phone continued to ring. I started wondering if Gino's was closed on Saturday, which struck me as odd. Every haircut I had been forced to get as a kid had taken place on a Saturday afternoon. I knew that dentists never worked on Fridays, and art galleries were closed Mondays, and you couldn't buy a car from a dealer on Sunday for love or money, but I didn't think barbers were that ridiculous. Saturday is the day people are free to do things they hate. Why wouldn't a barber work on Saturday?

The rings kept coming. I got the message. My right arm relaxed and performed the normal hang-up. Neither Tony nor Gino were at the barbershop. Or else they just weren't answering the phone. But why wouldn't anybody answer a telephone? As far as I knew I was the only person on earth who didn't answer telephones.

But the call hadn't told me what I wanted to know. Anybody could have called from the Bombalini household. I felt like mailing the three bills back to Tony and staying away from east Denver for the rest of my life. I examined that idea from every angle and decided it was "do-able." But Tony knew where I worked—and so did Uncle Gino.

I got into my cab and pulled back onto Colfax and headed east. I had a clammy feeling in my gut, generated by the fact that I was about to get drawn deeper into the personal lives of not only people, but people I didn't really know. Ironically, those are the kinds of people I like best. I wish I didn't know anybody. I would get along better with them.

I turned left onto Colorado Boulevard and cut up to 17th, turned right, and drove along a tree-lined street that had a fancy parkway. In my history class at UCD, the professor told us that the parkways in Denver were constructed where the rich people lived because the rich people controlled the City Council in the olden days, and the rich people wanted grassy parkways dividing the streets down the middle. The wider the parkways, the richer the people. Monaco Parkway is a monster. Whenever I encounter a narrow parkway with a thin strip of grass running five or six blocks I imagine the old money laughing at the nouveaux riches with their scrawny dividers. Does parkway-envy obsess nitwits in other cities? I had become especially conscious of parkways after I started hacking because I drove along them so often. I always see people jogging along the parkways at dawn. I don't know if old money still rules the City Council, but occasionally I see rich-looking women on Rollerblades gripping leashes while being towed bodily by golden retrievers. That's my kind of jogging.

I turned right onto Tony's street. The Mercedes was parked in the driveway. I was hoping there might be two cars. I was hoping Tony was home. Maybe he was in there right now waiting for me to knock on the door. I thought about pulling up at the curb and honking. Honking is improper protocol in the taxi business, but especially in rich neighborhoods. My rule of thumb is to never honk in a neighborhood where the residents enjoy a higher income bracket than myself, so as you might surmise, I don't do a lot of honking.

I pulled up in front of Tony's house and parked. I didn't bother to look at myself in the rear-view mirror as I usually do before approaching a house. Somehow I didn't think my hair and teeth really mattered that day. I climbed out of the cab and walked up the sidewalk, hoping the door would open before I got there. This sometimes happens. People seem to go on red alert when waiting for a cab driver to show up, as if they think a wealthy industrialist is going to kick down their door if they don't get a move on. That's one illusion I never tamper with.

I knocked on the door and waited, my ears ringing, my gut clammy, my breath shallow. I felt like I was waiting for the 15 bus.

The door opened and Mrs. Bombalini appeared before me. She smiled. "You must be Murph," she said, her irises rising and focusing on my shag.

I nodded.

"Please come in," she said in a well modulated, almost musical tone of voice.

I got rattled and began pointing at the cab with my thumb. "I'm just here to pick up a fare, ma'am, so if you're ready to go I do have kind of a really tight schedule to keep."

"Tony told me all about you," she said. "Won't you please come inside?"

Images of Lizzie Borden strafed my mind. I took a few steps back and shook my head no or yes, I don't remember.

"If you have a moment to spare, I need to speak with you," she said. She stepped onto the stoop and closed the door behind her. This had a calming effect. She was smaller than me, so I figured I could outrun her.

By now she was standing within arm's length of me. Her head was poised at a slight tilt, arms akimbo, as if she was studying something that she did not know existed anywhere on earth.

As my adrenaline levels dropped, she herself came into better focus. She was dressed like June Cleaver, pearls in the afternoon, with a dress that shimmered in lilac tones. And she was wearing high heels. My Maw would have pegged her as an Avon Lady. But she was just a regular housewife whose husband cut heads. My eyes kept flickering up to her blonde tippi-top. I was getting nothing but friendly vibes from Mrs. Bombalini. Why was I so afraid? I had once been a soldier. I suppose I have a tendency to lose my perspective at inconvenient moments. In the army I never got nailed for doing things that ought to have made me feel guilty but didn't. I could run real fast in the army.

"I have a feeling you don't need a taxi," I said, proud of my revived perspective.

She smiled and nodded. "You are correct about that," she said. "The reason I called your taxi company and asked for you personally is to find out if you have spoken to my husband since Thursday afternoon."

"No, ma'am," I blurted out before my Univac had a chance to spit.

She nodded and bit her lower lip, and bowed her head for a moment. When she looked up at me, her eyes were beginning to glisten with tears. But she blinked the thin film of moisture away and smiled at me.

"Could I talk you into coming into my home for a cup of coffee?" she said. "I'll pay you for your time."

This was far, far worse than being yelled at. I started to tell her that she didn't have to pay me for my time, but instead I remained silent, though not out of greed. For the second time that week I had simply decided it was time to shut up—and in both instances it was in the presence of a member of the Bombalini family.

Angelina offered me a seat in a kind of second living room at the rear of the house, which had a picture window with a sliding door that led out to a large, well-manicured backyard. She poured me a cup of coffee from a silver decanter. I was seated on the edge of a chair that might have been upholstered in silk, but I wasn't sure. I had spent my life farting through denim.

"My husband and I have been having financial difficulties lately," Mrs. Bombalini said, setting the decanter down and picking up her own cup. She took a sip. "My husband keeps reassuring me that everything is going to turn out all right, but our finances are getting to be a small problem. It's not terribly serious right now, but I'm afraid things might get worse. We have a few debts. They are not large, but debts tend to grow quickly." I sat silently and listened to this narrative just as I had listened to Tony on the previous Tuesday. I was on a brand-new spaceship and I intended to ride it all the way to the edge of the solar system if that's where Mrs. Bombalini wanted to go.

"Tony told me about hiring you to follow me last Tuesday," she said.

There went Mars again.

"After he spoke to you on the phone Thursday evening, he came home and confronted me. He said he had become suspicious after trying to get in touch with me in the daytime when I ought to have been at home. He said he had begun following me. Tony is a very jealous man. But he was afraid I was going to leave him, especially after our financial troubles began."

Mrs. Bombalini set her cup down and folded her hands on her lap. "You see, Murph, on those days that I was out of the house, I was looking for a job."

Hello Jupiter, goodbye Jupiter.

"Tony doesn't want me to have a job. Tony has worked hard all his life, and he has made good investments. There is more to it than that, of course. This house, and the Mercedes in the driveway, were gifts from his Uncle Gino. Gino has no children of his own. He's a bachelor. He coddles the two of us. He has been a barber for more than forty years. He is very well-to-do. Tony and I are well off, but I don't believe we would be living here if we had to pay for these things ourselves. Tony has always intended to pay Uncle Gino back, but I doubt if Gino would accept any money from

Tony. That's how the two of them are." She paused a moment and shrugged with a whimsical smile. "They're Italians," she said, as if that explained everything. You be the judge.

Mrs. Bombalini looked down at her hands folded on her lap, then looked up at me. "My husband has a gambling problem," she said. "That's the reason we are having financial difficulties. Tony is gambling away our money."

I raised my cup and took a long sip of coffee that had cooled considerably during her narrative. I lowered the cup a few inches and stared at her, but unlike last Tuesday I did not remark that I had no idea why she was telling me these things. The last time I did that was what had gotten me into this mess.

"So I called you here today, Murph, because I would like to hire you to follow my husband."

We passed Pluto and headed out into the void.

CHAPTER 18

"He can't help himself," Mrs. Bombalini said. "He lies about where the money goes. He works hard to earn the money, but then he tries to make more by betting. But he denies it. When he confronted me with his accusations, I finally told him I was trying to find a job to supplement my household income. He was shocked. He didn't expect that. He told me before we got married that he would be the breadwinner in this household. He doesn't want me to have a job. We argued today, and he walked out. He said he was going to the shop to work on the books."

I frowned at Mrs. Bombalini, then set my cup on the table. "I called the barbershop a little while ago," I said. "Nobody answered."

She nodded. "He's probably at the dog track. I find receipts from the track in his coat on occasion. They're always dated on Saturdays. He tells me that he's going to the shop to do the accounting, but then he goes to the track. That's where most of our money goes. I'm afraid to ask him if he goes to the mountain towns where gambling is legal. Lord knows how much he would lose in a casino. I hate to see him even buy scratch tickets. I don't know—it just seems so out of character for a man to work so hard to earn money and then throw it away on lottery tickets."

"They say it's a disease," I said. That's my excuse anyway.

She nodded. "I'm so alone in this. That's why I called you, Murph. Your willingness to help Tony indicated to me that you might be of help to me."

"Can I ask you something?" I said to change the subject as fast as humanly possible.

"Certainly."

"When I followed you on Thursday, you went into the Strand Building. Were you applying for a job there?"

"Yes I was. There's a large boutique that sells designer fans in the Strand. I was hoping to get a job as a sales clerk in their showroom. But they aren't hiring right now."

"Were the fans blowing in the showroom?"

"Yes. It was like a wind tunnel."

That would explain the disheveled look. But what about the bar? "Did you apply for a job at The Cherry Pit?" I said.

She lowered her eyes. "I felt so foolish after going in there. I was a waitress in college. I know how to do it. But when I entered the bar, I met two women with whom I am acquainted. They had stopped at The Cherry Pit for a few drinks after shopping. I knew then that I could never work there. It upset me to realize how desperate I was becoming. I didn't apply for the job."

I finally had to ask. "What were you doing at the Hilton?"

"There's a gift shop in the Hilton. I had put in an application to work there last week. But they told me they didn't need anyone at the moment."

Shop girl. Waitress. Jaysus ... waitress. How could I turn down an ex-waitress?

"Why do you want me to follow Tony?" I said.

"I just want to know if he went to the dog track today. I want to know if he's betting a lot of money. I want to be able to confront him with this. I'm going to try to get him into Gambler's Anonymous. I need somebody who is good at following people without their knowing it, and you're the only person I know who does that."

"If I find Tony at the dog track, do you want me to talk to him about his betting?" I said.

"No. I just want to know if he's there, and how much he bets. I want to be able to tell him that I know everything. I want to be able to confront him with the truth. I would go to the track myself, but I'm not sure either of us could deal with a scene like that."

I'm not sure the owners of the track could either. I've been to the dog track plenty of times. Big Al showed me the ropes. Race tracks are mellow places in spite of the lurid rep manufactured by guys like Damon Runyan. The people who go to dog tracks are as polite as anybody I met at Dyna-Plex. And probably as desperate.

"I'll be glad to go out to the track and take a look," I said. "And you don't have to pay me anything, ma'am. Your husband has already paid me plenty." Suddenly the three bills didn't seem so dirty anymore. Thank God for abstract concepts.

I stayed a few more minutes. We discussed some of the details, how I would contact her again and so forth. She told me she intended to bring Uncle Gino in on the intervention. I'm glad she mentioned him. I thought she might want me around when she confronted Tony with the facts, but I didn't want to be anywhere near Gino when that scene came down. He looked like a man who knew how to use a broomstick—and how to find one if he didn't have one. I planned to be nowhere near the action when it started. That was another lesson I learned in the army.

I pulled away from the house and headed west toward Colorado Boulevard, feeling rather lightheaded. In fact, I felt somewhat like an automaton again, doing things I didn't want to do but doing them anyway. I turned north on Colorado. This would take me to Vasquez Boulevard, which in turn would take me all the way north to Commerce City where the kennel club was located. I knew the route well. I once picked up a fare in south Denver near County Line Road and drove all the way through heavy traffic to the dog track without hitting a single red light, a distance of more than ten miles. It was a bravura performance of taxi driving that my fare didn't seem to appreciate. He tipped me a buck.

But as I drove to the track that day in search of Tony, I appreciated every red light I hit. I was hoping the electric power grid in America would fail, and a traffic jam of gargantuan proportions would prevent me from arriving. I wanted another Trip From Hell.

All right. Here's my Vail story:

One winter morning I picked up two young couples at the old Stapleton International Airport who had come to Colorado to make the ski resort scene. I had to put four sets of skis inside my taxi, placed at an angle across the tops of the seatbacks, with the tips pressed against the back window. This is how all cab drivers do skis if they don't have a rack on the roof. Passengers sit with skis near their faces all the way to the resort. Roughing it, but in a fun way if you get my drift. The couples were young, from the East, and had been drinking on the airplane. They were having a good time. I was given one hundred dollars cash up front. That was a big score in those days.

I reported my fare to the dispatcher, and told him I would be gone the rest of the day. The dispatcher wished me a good trip, and I headed for I-70 that would take me up into the mountains. The day was clear, and relatively warm for a December. But by the time we made it up into the mountains, a cloud cover had formed. Pretty soon a light snow was falling. I wasn't worried. My taxi had good snow tires for the winter season and I had a full tank of gas.

By the time we were halfway to Vail the snowflakes had gotten big, but the roads were still clear. Traffic was heavy. Most of the cars on the road had skis on their roof racks. Skiing baffles me even more than golf. I deliberately avoid all activities that involve standing up.

A full-tilt blizzard eventually settled over the Front Range. My fares were ecstatic. The skiing looked good. The two young men in the group kept saying that they couldn't wait to get out on the slopes and "catch some wind," whatever that meant. I was subjected to a detailed lecture on the glories of wax ski boots, whatever they are. The couples broke out a pint of Southern Comfort and began passing it back and forth with my permission. This was against the law, but we were in the high country, and as Burt Reynolds yells in *Deliverance,* "What law!" I was hoping the perky couples would drink themselves into unconsciousness, but they made it to Vail okay. After we unloaded the baggage at the hotel, the drunk boys slipped me fifteen bucks each as a tip.

Vail was as far as I got that day. By then the Front Range was snowbound. I couldn't get out of town. It took me four hours to find a motel with a vacancy. It was the kind of motel that skiers do not patronize. Let's just say it was rustic. Let's just say it was off the main thoroughfare, down a dirt road near a frozen creek. That night's stay cost me thirty bucks.

The next day it was still snowing. I made my way back to Vail only to learn from a State Patrolman that the road to Denver was shut down to all traffic, including snowplows. I was trapped in the mountains for three days. When I finally got back to Denver, Hogan took pity on me and charged me only a two-day lease. My profits for my trip came to zero. It was actually less than zero, even though math professors tell us that in the real world there are no such things as negative numbers—but I know different.

End of story.

I connected with Vasquez Boulevard and headed northeast along the highway. Vasquez cuts through vast industrial flats, a bleak and unscenic part of the metro area. A lot of semi-tractor trailers use this route. There's lots of junkyards. I once visited one of the junkyards. A few years before I started driving a taxi, I was an assistant maintenance man in a plastics factory. The maintenance man was an alcoholic in his early fifties, a skinny guy whose hands trembled whenever he handled electrical wiring. He wasn't very skillful. He got shocked a lot. He was always hungover. He drove a beat-up station wagon filled with soft-core pornography. Whenever he sent me out to his heap to retrieve one tool or another, I took a glance at the skin mags.

One time he told me to go to his toolbox and get the plumb bob. I thought he was kidding. I thought he was treating me like a "new guy" and was sending me on a snipe hunt. I had never heard the term "plumb bob" before. I just stood there grinning at him. Again he told me to go out to his car and get the plumb bob. I finally said, "What's a plumb bob?" as if I was part of a vaudeville act. I expected him to break up laughing and admit there was no such thing. But instead he got irritated at me. He was somewhat of a wreck of a human being, so I could tell he was happy to find a person even more pathetic than himself. He described the device to me, and I went out and got the plumb bob. If you've never heard of a plumb bob before, it's a metal thing with a string on it, that's all I can say.

Anyway, one day the maintenance man sent me to a junkyard on Vasquez Boulevard to buy a concrete sink for the factory. I didn't know if new ones were too expensive, but I did learn one thing: they weighed a ton. The junkyard had exactly one concrete sink. Me and a black clerk hauled it to the station wagon on a dolly, then we had to lift it into the rear where all the porno was lying scattered about. But I had forgotten to set the car in park or something because when we hoisted it up to the rear, the station wagon started rolling forward. That's how heavy the sink was. We almost dropped the damn thing. I had to run to the driver's side and hit the emergency brake.

The sink was so heavy that the station wagon sat real low to the ground. The wheels looked squashed. I asked the clerk if he thought it was safe to drive the station wagon with so much weight in the rear, and he said, "Not if you drive as reckless as you park."

I guided the station wagon slowly down Vasquez with the front wheels barely touching the road. The front end drifted from side to side. It was like flying an airplane. Somehow I made it to the plastics factory. The next day I didn't go back to work. I never returned to the factory. Instead, I applied to UCD so I could start receiving GI Bill checks from the government to sit in a classroom and do nothing until I graduated. My trip along Vasquez Boulevard to the dog track reminded me of The Day Of The Concrete Sink, the day I kissed manual labor goodbye forever. I credit my English degree to that sink.

The kennel club came into view. When you saw it from a distance, you felt like you were approaching the Roman Coliseum. It's a white wooden stadium that towers over the Commerce City flats. The parking lot was filled almost to capacity. I had to park at the farthest edge of the lot. I got out and walked to the gate, passed through the turnstile, and stopped at a vendor to buy a tip-sheet—the schedule of dogs running that day. But I didn't plan to use the sheet for its intended purpose, which was to calculate the most efficient way to lose money. I intended to hide my face from Tony Bombalini.

CHAPTER 19

I took the stairs up to the clubhouse where the betting windows were located. The clubhouse of the dog track is a nice clean family place, with a vast concrete floor covered with small tables where bettors can sit and make their calculations and watch the races on TVs mounted high on pillars. There are snack stands here and there. You can buy beer and soft drinks, potato chips, the works. People were milling about, waiting for the next race to begin out on the track. I started my search in the clubhouse, peering over the top of my tip-sheet. It's a long walk from one end of the clubhouse to the other, as long as the length of the track outside.

My eyeballs moved side to side, studying fifty-foot quadrants of the floor. I had been trained in the army to scan the terrain this way to spot enemy troops, but I used it mostly to spot bars.

Then I saw him. Tony was seated at a table hunched over a tip-sheet and marking it with a pencil. His hunch was a familiar one. It was a desperation hunch.

I drifted over to a wall, watching Tony and waiting for him to get up and go to one of the betting windows. I decided to let a few people get behind him, then I would slip into the rear of the line and give his bet a listen. Whichever way he departed the window, left or right, I intended to go the other way and keep out of sight. My only hope lay in the fact that people who bet are so engulfed by the frantic thoughts racing around the cindertrack of their brains that they tend not to notice people around them. I wrote the book.

Then I saw Big Al.

He was seated alone at a table in the middle of the crowd. He wasn't hunched over even though he was working a tip-sheet. The pencil in his right hand was wiggling. He was crossing out the losers and circling the winners. I had seen him do this on many occasions. Big Al had introduced me to the dog track years ago, and after the first season at the track he advised me to stick with cab driving.

Keeping an eye on Tony, I eased my way through the throng, making my way toward Big Al. I pulled out a chair and sat down across from him.

He glanced up at me, then looked back down at his tip-sheet and kept on scribbling. "What's popping, weekend-lease?" he said.

The Word was out. Murph was working hard. I looked at his wiggling pencil. He was making notes on a small square of paper. By "notes" I mean numbers. Big Al was a numbers man. He was the exact opposite of me.

He paused a moment and flipped the pencil, erased a number, then put the lead back against the paper. "You must have dropped a fare off in the parking lot," Big Al said, "because I just know you didn't come here to bet. What did I tell you about sticking with cab driving?"

"I'm not here to bet," I said.

He grunted his approval and kept on scribbling.

I licked my lips and glanced at Tony, who was holding the palm of his right hand over his mouth the way you do to wipe away a milk mustache. I looked at Big Al and licked my lips again, then scooted the chair closer to the table.

"Big Al," I said. "If I were to ask you to do me a favor with no questions asked, would you do it?"

"Yeah."

He kept scribbling.

"Do you see that man in the black coat seated at the table over by the wall?"

Big Al glanced to his right, then looked back at his notes. "Yeah."

"He's a friend of mine. He's got troubles. I need to know what kind of bets he's making. Could you follow him to the window and find out for me?"

"Yeah."

Big Al kept scribbling. He didn't look at me and he didn't look at Tony again. He didn't ask questions. He just sat there making numbers. I started to wonder if he had heard a word I'd said. Bettors can get that way and stay that way to the bitter end of the last race.

Tony got up from his chair and started toward a window, and Big Al suddenly stood up and walked quickly across the floor carrying his tip-sheet. He got in line behind Tony. Big Al has the best peripheral vision at Rocky Cab.

I put my left elbow on the table and hid my face with my left hand, but I couldn't do much about my shag. I gazed at the top of the table the way losers gaze at things.

I heard a chair scrape. I looked up and saw Big Al dropping his tip-sheet onto the table. He sat down. "Your friend is betting long-shots," he said. "He's going down."

"Did he bet a lot?"

"Yeah."

"Should I ask how much?"

"Nah."

"That much, huh?"

"Yeah."

I sat back in my chair and sighed. I looked over at Tony, who was seated at his table again, studying the ticket stubs in his hand as though they might reveal the secret of winning big. He looked like a novelist trying to decipher the true meaning behind a rejection slip. I had found out every-thing Angelina Bombalini had wanted to know. Tony was here and he was betting big and losing big. Big Al may not have had the ability to predict every winner in a race, but he could spot a loser at a glance.

He glanced at me.

"You look worried, Tenderfoot."

I nodded. I wanted badly to tell Big Al what was going on, but there are some things in life you can't confess even to a cabbie.

Big Al looked at his wristwatch. Then he reached into his shirt pocket, pulled out three dollars, and handed them to me. "Go get yourself some liquid refreshment and meet me back here in forty-five minutes," he said.

Since this was a day of no-questions-asked, I took the money and stood up.

"And stay away from the beer," Big Al said. "You're on duty." How many times had my sergeants said that to me?

Well ... what's three-hundred sixty-five times two?

I pocketed the money and walked away from the table.

I headed toward a snack stand at the far end of the room where Tony wasn't likely to see me. I bought a Coke, then stepped over near a pillar and stood there, sipping. I scanned the room. I adjusted my glasses. Thank God for Sheila. I saw Big Al sitting at Tony's table now. I didn't know what he was doing, but he looked like he was regaling Tony, who appeared to be mesmerized by Big Al's spiel.

One of the nice things about a dog track is that everybody is friendly. They're all there for the same reason. It's like one big happy deluded family. You form brief friendships with total strangers, you exchange opinions, you congratulate or console, then you move on.

By now Big Al and Tony were hunched over a tip-sheet, and Big Al was jabbing at the page with an extended finger. I looked at my wristwatch. I decided to go outside and look at the dogs as they were being led into the starting gate for the next race. Some of the greyhounds were big, and some were little. The big ones tended to run faster, as I had learned. I had learned a lot of things under Big Al's tutelage. But the most important thing he had taught me about betting on the dogs was to stick with cab driving.

I took a seat on the bleachers and watched the race. The big dog won. I went back inside.

Tony and Big Al were standing at a betting window, chatting like old pals. I glanced at my wristwatch, then went for another Coke.

I stepped outside and watched another race. Big dog, ho hum. I went back inside and looked around the room but couldn't see Tony. I began drifting toward the table where I had first seen Big Al. I finally spotted him at a different table. I moved toward him, scouring the room for Tony, but I didn't see him anywhere.

I pulled out a chair and sat down.

"Your friend just won seventeen hundred dollars in the twin-quin," Big Al said. He was scribbling new numbers.

"Seventeen hundred?" I said.

He glanced up at me. "I advised him to take the money and run. He took it."

I just sat there with the cold cup in my hand. "How much did he bet?" I said.

"Twenty bucks."

"And he won seventeen hundred?"

"Yeah."

"Did you tell him what dogs to bet on?"

"Yeah."

"Did you win big, too?"

"Yeah."

I looked down at the Coke in my hand. Suddenly I wasn't thirsty anymore.

I set the cup down and looked at Big Al. "Why didn't you let me in on this magic act?"

Big Al finally sat back in his chair. He was folding a small sheet of paper into halves. He tucked it into his shirt pocket. "That was the guy who was asking about you at the Brown last Monday," he said. "I recognized him the moment you pointed him out to me."

I nodded as if he had asked me a question.

"Didn't I tell you never to get involved in the personal lives of your fares?"

I knew I had heard that somewhere before.

"But you just had to go and get involved, didn't you?"

I nodded, then said, "Did he tell you about me?"

"Hell no. But I can read you like an X-ray, Tenderfoot."

Big Al knew how to make me bristle. I had been driving a taxi for fourteen years. I was no tenderfoot.

Or was I?

"I don't know who that guy is or what his problems are, and I don't want to know," Big Al said, pulling out a blank sheet of paper. "Now, if you will excuse me, I must prepare for the trifecta."

He opened his tip-sheet and began scribbling numbers at the top of the page.

I scooted my chair back and stood up. "Thanks, Big Al," I said. He raised his pencil and gave it a couple twitches, then went back to scribbling. I turned and walked toward an exit. Tony was probably on his way home by now. I wanted to get to a phone and call Angelina to let her know that Tony had been at the track. I wasn't going to tell her about Tony's win. I would let Tony do that. But I couldn't see a phone anywhere. I finally walked up to a security guard, a tall, lean black man who was standing at parade rest, his hands crossed behind his back. His chin was raised and he was scanning the crowd.

"Excuse me, sir," I said. "Can you tell me where there's a public telephone around here?"

He glanced at me. Then he frowned. It was the deepest frown that I had ever seen on the face of any human being.

"What are you talking about?" he said. "There ain't no public telephones at the dog track."

"No telephones?" I said.

"No telephones," he said. "So if you want to call your buddies, you got to go outside and find a telephone at a gas station where you can't see the tote board."

I backed away. "Thank you, sir," I said. I turned and headed for the stairwell that would take me downstairs and out to the real world where telephones existed, where there was water in the faucets and electricity in the wires, and all mankind lived without fear of peculiar rules.

I drove back down Vasquez Boulevard. I passed gas stations where public telephones were located, but I didn't stop. Partly it was ennui, but mostly I had the idea that since I was going back to Denver anyway, I might as well make a run past the Bombalini house. I suspected that a seventeen-hundred-dollar win in the twin-quin would ameliorate some of the tensions wrought by Tony's gambling. I know a little bit about amelioration. I won a twin-quin during my first season at the dog track. I raked in eight hundred bucks one Friday night. I spent the following two days getting completely ameliorated. I barely made it to work on Monday.

For those of you who don't know what a twin-quin is, it's a twin-quinella. I don't know what the translation of "quinella" is, but I believe it's Italian. I've always wondered why the people of Italy don't speak Latin. In English a twin-quin means you pick the first- and second-place dogs in two consecutive races—four winning dogs. The odds are slim, which is why the payoff is so big. I won my TQ after Big Al taught me how to properly read a tip-sheet. It was like studying algebra. I spent Thursday night cramming for the Friday exam. I picked the right dogs and pocketed eight hundred bucks.

That was my downfall—winning.

It seemed so easy that I went back to the track every night the following week. I blew a bundle trying to win another twin-quin. I couldn't stop myself from making bets. My eight hundred bucks was being whittled away. I had a monkey on my back. I had a foot in a birdcage. I was turning into a dog track junkie, a greyhound hop-head. Big Al knew I was going down. He finally held an intervention. He took me aside and said, "Stick with cab driving, Tenderfoot."

I've been straight ever since. Not counting scratch tickets.

When I got to 17th Avenue I turned left and cruised past the Rollerbladers until I got to Tony's street. I didn't go all the way down the street. I looked for two cars. I didn't see two. I didn't know what kind of car Tony drove and I didn't especially want to know. It might have been a Rolls, and I wasn't sure I could take that. But the Mercedes was the only car in the driveway. I didn't know what to make of this. I pulled a discreet U-turn at the end of the block, keeping an eye out for cops. This traffic violation was similar to parking in a no-parking zone. The fact that I was actually inside my taxi while making the U-turn didn't reassure me.

I drove back up to 17th wondering if I should go ahead and find a phone and call Mrs. Bombalini. I wondered if I should tell her about Tony's big win. I wondered why Tony wasn't there. I wondered why I had gotten involved in a fare's personal life. I wondered why I hadn't listened to Big Al. I wondered if Big Al was wondering the same thing. I wondered why I wondered about that.

I decided to head back into the city and check out the hotels. As Big Al had said, I was on duty, and I still had to earn the rent for this month. It was getting on toward five o'clock, and Denver Saturday night was just beginning. I turned on the Rocky radio and started listening for bells. I figured I would wait until six P.M. before calling Mrs. Bombalini. That's when most of the afternoon losers would be home from the dog track. It would give me another hour to pretend that everything was okay. Pretense has always been my life's blood, and as Janis Joplin used to shriek, *"... Get it while you can!!! ..."*

CHAPTER 20

I headed west past City Park listening to the traffic on the radio and holding my microphone in my right hand. You have to hold the mike when the competition is fierce. The second or two that it takes to grab it off the dashboard and press the button is the difference between going home flush and just going home. All the old pros have their mikes in their hands on Saturday night.

I passed Grant Street and started down the hill to Broadway when the radio suddenly barked, "L-5 Brown Palace!" I sailed down the hill and swung a left onto Tremont and saw the most beautiful sight a cab driver can see: a crowd of people with luggage waiting on the sidewalk and no cabs in sight. I glanced in my rear-view mirror and saw two taxis racing around the corner behind me. The locusts were descending. I drove up to the door and hopped out. The doorman helped me with the luggage, herded my two passengers into the backseat, and plucked his tip. By the time I was back in the driver's seat there were seven cabs behind me and plenty of fares waiting at the curb. I sailed away to the tune of "Airport!" sung by a man seated next to a woman in my backseat. I decided to assume they were married. In the cab-driving game, as in creative writing, you always go from the general to the specific.

Fifty bucks guaranteed. I felt happy. This was so much better than playing the dogs. I made idle chatter with my fares on the way out. The man asked how long I had been driving a taxi. Fourteen years I told him. You get the same questions all the time. He was wearing a nice suit. I had him pegged as a junior exec. His wife never said anything, she just sat there with a pleased smile, gazing at the passing landscape—two happy people going to the airport. I myself am never happy when I have to catch a plane. I hate flying. I've had to do that on a few occasions in my life, most often in the army. It's not that I don't trust airplanes. I don't trust air.

I was so pleased about scoring a DIA trip on a Saturday evening that I made a mistake. When I got to the airport I was so busy lying to the man about what a swell day I was having that I took the wrong ramp up to the terminal. Cab drivers are required to let their passengers off on Ramp 3, but I drove them up to Ramp 4 and didn't even realize it until I was unloading their luggage. I noticed that there didn't seem to be any other taxis around, and suddenly I realized I was violating the rules!

Violating rules has never bothered me much, but if a cop catches a cabbie on Ramp 4, he will write him a ticket on the spot. The cops are brutal at DIA. They pop out of nowhere. If a civilian leaves his car unattended for ten seconds, a tow truck pops out of nowhere, too. The cops have a hard job, which is to keep the traffic flowing in front of the terminal, and they're relentless. The penalty for a cab dropping fares off on Ramp 4 is fifty dollars, non-negotiable.

My heart started pounding. I raced to get the luggage to the curb, then waited anxiously while the man counted out the bills and handed them to me. I thanked him and dashed to my cab and hopped in, stomped on the accelerator, and got the hell out of there, watching in my rear-view mirror for cops. It was a miracle. I got away with it, but my palms were sweating. I had talked to plenty of cab drivers who had erred when DIA first opened. They would drive down to the cab staging area mad as hell, waving their tickets and trying to drum up sympathy from the other drivers, most of whom found it funny. There are few things in this world as humiliating as getting nailed by an authentic personal screw-up. I wrote the book. My book states that mankind's greatest fear is not death, but humiliation. Some people would rather die than be laughed at. I don't want to get grotesque here, but I can think of a lot of things worse than death, many of which I have experienced first hand.

But it's always difficult to counter the effects of being humiliated in public. Kids learn a rudimentary form of retaliation on the school playground, utilizing such tactics as "Oh yeah?" as well as the ever-popular, "Sez you!"

Teenagers often go to fists, and while this offers a certain amount of personal gratification, it really doesn't address the issue. You never quite get over the feeling that the other teens at the soda shop are laughing at you behind your back. You become sullen and resentful, which often provokes acts of inexplicable behavior bordering on psychosis, such as joining the army.

Fortunately, my years of taxi driving have helped me to develop a defensive technique that I refer to as "hu-jitsu" or "humiliation-jitsu." This is where you use the momentum of the attack to your advantage. Rather than try to counter an assault of laughter by standing firm and fending off your opponent with brute force, you simply say to yourself, "He's right. I'm an idiot." The near miss, on the other hand, is a more subtle problem. Almost getting nailed can sometimes be worse than getting nailed because it generates a condition of "self-doubt." That's why my palms were sweating as I drove down the highway heading to Denver. I had an empty feeling inside me, caused by the knowledge that I had a made a critical error in the one aspect of my existence where I had long considered myself to be somewhat of an expert, which is cab driving. When I had realized that I was on Ramp 4, I felt like I was in some kind of a bizarre dream. It was like my dream of going down to Rocky and taking a cab without authorization and driving around Denver just waiting to get nailed. The caliber of the mistake was so overwhelmingly amateurish that I felt humiliated even though there was nobody laughing at me—not even myself, which is rare.

It made me feel so stupid, and even somewhat despondent, that I had a sudden, almost grievous need to set things right, and this was what made me pull off the highway to find a 7-11 in Aurora and call Mrs. Bombalini. I felt that if I got this chore out of the way, all would be right with the world. This wasn't an entirely unprecedented approach to despondency. For instance, back in college whenever I had a severe hangover I would do my laundry. Go figure.

I took I-225 down to the Colfax exit and got off. There was a 7-11 near the intersection. I pulled in and climbed out of my cab. I looked at my wristwatch. It was ten minutes to six. I found a phone that wasn't too badly damaged and dialed the Bombalini household. At that point I didn't care if Gino picked up at the other end. I just wanted to talk to someone in that family, get it said, and get it over with.

"Hello?"

It was Mrs. Bombalini.

"Hello, this is Murph. Did Tony get home yet?"

"No, Murph, he hasn't come home. Did you see him at the dog track?"

I hesitated. I felt like I had been caught in a lie, which is not an uncommon reaction to almost everything I ever say to everybody. Consequently I was able to calm myself down and focus. "Yes I did," I said. "He was there making bets. But he left before the start of the last race. I didn't talk to him or anything. I assumed he would be home by now."

"No, he hasn't arrived," she said. She sounded resigned, as if she was used to Tony's peccadilloes. "Were you able to determine whether he was making large bets?"

I hesitated again. I did not want to draw Big Al into this scenario. I had never actually crossed Big Al in any major way, and this had "major" written all over it. "From what I was able to determine, Tony was betting long shots. That's not a good way to bet."

There was a moment of silence at the other end of the line. Then she said, "Did you follow him after he left the track?"

The next series of lie/truths came so easily that I was almost proud of myself as I articulated them. "My cab was parked way at the far edge of the parking lot. The lot is really big. I didn't know where Tony was parked." I stopped to see if she would follow this line of "reasoning" all the way to its erroneous conclusion. I had my fingers crossed.

"Well, Tony hasn't come home yet," she said, as if she was already past that and thinking about other things. I felt a tremendous burden lifted from my shoulders. But then she said, "Did he win anything?"

Suddenly the telephone box turned into Big Al's face. The receiver turned into Big Al's hand reaching for my throat. I held the receiver away from my neck for a moment, then swallowed hard. There was only one thing to do—be evasive. I had found this is to be an effective alternative to everything.

"I ... don't ... know," I said as clearly and decisively as Jon Voight said in *Deliverance* when he lied his ass off to James Dickey.

There was another moment of deliberation at the other end of the line, then Mrs. Bombalini said, "Well, I suppose he will be home any time now. He always comes home. Thank you so much for doing this for me, Murph. I really would like to pay you for your time."

"No please, that's all right, Mrs. Bombalini. I was happy to do it."

"Well ... all right. I have to hang up now. I'm right in the middle of preparing dinner. Thank you for everything, Murph."

"You're welcome."

"Goodbye."

"Goodbye."

Goodbye. Goodbye. Goodbye Mrs. Bombalini and your desperate husband who bets long shots and gives away free haircuts and pays cabbies three hundred dollars to feed his paranoia. When I hung up the phone I felt as if I had not made a phone call at all. Nothing had changed inside me. I went back to my taxi and sat in the driver's seat and stared at the facade of the 7-11. I felt the way Ned Beatty looked at the end of *Deliverance.*

I started the engine and backed out of the slot and drove onto Colfax listening to bells. There was a call at a King Soopers on Havana that nobody was jumping. I knew what it was: a shopper taking her groceries home. I knew what the fare would come to: five dollars. All supermarket bells came to five dollars. When I first started cab driving I worked the supermarkets for a couple of months because I could average twenty dollars an hour doing four trips. It nearly killed me.

I finally got out of the supermarket game and went into the hotel business where I could count on one trip an hour with plenty of time to read paperbacks.

But I went ahead and jumped the bell. The supermarket was a few miles farther along Colfax. When I pulled up I saw an elderly black woman standing beside her shopping cart. The cart was filled to the brim with white plastic bags. That's part of what nearly killed me in the old days, thousands upon thousands of white plastic bags going in and out of my trunk all day long. But on this night, after I opened my trunk for the woman, it felt good to have those bags in my hands again. I hadn't done this in years. It felt like I had returned to the days of my youth when four bells an hour seemed like a pot-o'-gold at the end of a rainbow, and I never got involved in the personal lives of my fares.

The meter came to four dollars. I carried her white plastic bags into her house. It took three trips. When I finished she handed me a dollar tip and said, "Thank you, little brother." She was really old.

I made my way back to Colfax and headed toward downtown, knowing that there was no quitting for the night. I wanted to quit though. I wanted to go back to my crow's nest, kick off my Keds, crawl into bed, and pull the covers over my head.

Pretty soon I was approaching Gino's Barbershop. I slowed as I passed. The CLOSED sign was on the door. The lights were out. I couldn't see anything inside. I didn't see any Rolls-Royce parked at the curb. I was sort of hoping that Tony would be there.

I cruised on past. I felt as if I was saying goodbye forever to the worst mess I had been in this month.

I kept driving, listening to the radio and not jumping bells that I could have. I was getting closer to the street where my crow's nest was located. I looked at my wristwatch. There was a whole night ahead of me, and I needed to make the rent. But I was lying to myself. The three hundred dollars that Tony had paid me would cover the rent. I had absolutely no reason whatsoever to keep on working. It was the dream of a lifetime. But I didn't stop. I rolled past the intersection that would have taken me home. I headed into downtown Denver where people were entering bars, catching movies and plays, seeking something that was missing from their lives on the weekdays, and scattering like ants all over the city. I would play the Saturday game. I would play it long and I would play it hard.

I drove to the Brown Palace and parked in line at the cabstand. I wanted to cool down, take a breather, and prepare myself mentally for "Anvil 2: The Sequel."

There were four taxis ahead of me. I reached into the backseat and pressed the lock on each of the rear doors. I vowed that if a pedestrian tried to ambush me, I would inform him that PUC forbade me from picking up fares who had not called the Rocky Mountain Taxicab Company ahead of time and made an appointment. If he tried to argue with me, I would tell him that none of the other cab companies in the city were covered by the regulation. This was both a risky and a cruel thing to do to the drivers in line because if any of them ever found out I had made a vow to direct pedestrians to their taxis, I would become what is known on the streets as a "vehicular outsider." In other words, I would be branded.

CHAPTER 21

I dropped off my last drunk at two-thirty A.M.

I drove straight back to my building and climbed up to my crow's nest. I shoved all my money into my *Finnegans* without bothering to count it, like Kenny Roger's gambler—the difference being that a cab driver who waits until the game is over to count his money might find himself scrambling to pick up a couple more fares before heading back to the motor.

As I said, a cabbie is like a quarterback keeping an eye on the clock, but if you get smug and take your eye off the clock, you can lose control of the game. I didn't feel smug that night, but I did take my eye off the clock. I was now taking a long time-out. I had a weekend lease, so keeping tabs on how much money I had earned wasn't critical at the moment. I still had all day Sunday to meet both of my goals, which was to make the rent and avoid people for the rest of my life.

I slept lousy that night. They say there's no rest for the wicked, but I had never had any trouble sleeping before. I sometimes fall asleep in my taxi outside hotels, only to be awakened by the starting of other cab engines, as well as the frantic beeping of horns behind me. Newbies, of course. You can always spot the newbies. They honk impatiently when the only place they're going is one space forward. They're like cops at the DIA terminal, trying to keep everything organized. Newbies like that don't last long. Anyone who tries to organize cabbies is in for a rude awakening.

The problem resides in the fact that cab driving is not only one of the last bastions of true free enterprise, it's also one of the last bastions of old-fashioned Yankee chaos. Cab drivers on the whole don't dress very snazzy, and not all cabbies speak proper English, including some of the foreigners.

Cabbies have their own views on politics, religion, and sports, the three most dangerous intersections in the city. If cab drivers were interested in conformity, they would be bus drivers. I don't know how rugged the average cab driver is, but I have never met one who wasn't an individualist. We're all the same.

Just for your info, Denver taxi licenses historically have always been referred to as "Herdic" licenses. Don't ask me why. Denver history interests me, but not that much.

I woke up in the middle of the morning unable to get back to sleep, wondering if Tony had made it home from the track. It was no longer any of my business, but the fact that something is none of my business has nothing to do with my life. I tossed and turned, and finally fell into a fitful slumber around nine A.M.

I woke up again at eleven A.M. and crawled out of the sack. There was no use going for my normal ten hours of sleep. I would just have to settle for a lousy eight. I would be sipping a lot of joe that day.

It felt strange to be working on a Sunday. The streets were deserted. I felt like the Omega Man. Since I didn't get on the road until almost noon, I missed the church rush, if there is such a thing. You hear rumors. Throughout my Wichita childhood, I had never seen a member of Blessed Virgin parish arrive in a taxi. Somehow I don't think Monsignor O'Leary would have approved of the cost. Among middle-class citizens, taxis are generally used only for emergencies, so anybody who needs to get to church that badly might want to consider self-flagellation.

The only emergencies I've ever been involved with were midnight runs to liquor stores, and childbirth. I've delivered three babies since I first began driving a taxi. I'm not going to tell you the details. I don't even remember the details of the first delivery. I was informed later that the mother and baby were taken by ambulance to the maternity ward at Denver General Hospital. I myself was wheeled into the emergency ward.

The second and third deliveries went more smoothly. By that time I had figured out what to do with an umbilical cord. I've also been involved with lesser medical emergencies. It's kind of unsettling to find yourself dealing with people in actual physical distress when all you want out of life is be left alone forever. But like a draftee who becomes a medic in a war, I made the necessary attitude adjustment. I charge an extra twenty cents a mile for broken bones—but appendectomies are negotiable.

I listened to both the AM radio and the Rocky radio that Sunday, taking every bell I could grab. The town wasn't hopping but the fares added up. Sunday evenings can be good for airport runs, so at four o'clock I started hanging around the hotels. At five I copped a DIA out of the Fairmont, and that put me over the top as far as my rent was concerned.

After I dropped off the fare, I cruised down to the staging area just to take a look. I instinctively dislike deadheading, and I figured if there weren't many cabs waiting I might try it. When I got to the area I saw only a dozen or so taxis. This put me into a quandary. Not a moral quandary, just a regular one. The line was short, which made it enticing, but this was a Sunday and I might find myself waiting three hours for twelve taxis to move. It was a gamble, and I didn't take it. It had been a long weekend, and while I wasn't tired I decided to quit while I was behind. As I said, I had learned long ago that you never get ahead in this game. There's always tomorrow. I still had six hours left on my lease, but I deadheaded back to the motor and turned in 127.

That was the end of that week.

CHAPTER 22

I had made my rent and I was due for my monthly spring break. Spring break at Murph's Cabaña can last anywhere from three to nine days, depending on how bored I get lying on a bath towel on my living room floor reading paperbacks—"unwinding" as the psychotherapists call it.

When I got into my crow's nest on Sunday night I turned on the TV and cooked a hamburger. I was down to my last white dot. This meant that on Monday I would have to do my shopping, which put a damper on my vacation. I intensely dislike doing anything at all, such as brushing my teeth, or shaving, or even tying my Keds, since those little chores add up to wasted minutes when I could be doing nothing. So shopping was kind of The Big Grind in my life. But I tried to put it out of my mind because there was nothing I could do about it. Food is like money: you can live with it, but you can't live without it.

There was something else grinding at me that evening as I watched Mary Ann put her fists on her hips and roll her eyes with exasperation as Gilligan did something to bug her—I don't know what since I never look at him when Mary Ann is onstage. Ironically, I never take my eyes off Maynard G. Krebs when I catch an old *Dobie Gillis* show on cable. I watched Dobie first run when I was a boy in Wichita, and the show struck me as the most sophisticated and intellectually satisfying production on television. Nothing's changed. Bob Denver truly defined the parameters of broadcast entertainment in the twentieth century from the sublime to the ridiculous. Parameters fascinate me. I could use a few in my life.

The thing that was grinding at me though was the sense that I still had not earned the three bills that were stuck in my *Finnegans*. I couldn't stop wondering about Tony. I kept thinking I should give Mrs. Bombalini another call and find out what was up. Surely Tony had made it back home. But whether he did or did not was no longer my concern. Nevertheless, I felt like a cabbie who had pulled up at his destination and turned around only to discover that his fare had disappeared from the backseat. A kind of *Twilight Zone* deal—unfinished business, if you get my drift.

I tried to concentrate on the TV, which was not difficult. When I was a kid, concentrating on homework was difficult—concentrating on TV is about as difficult as concentrating on self-pity.

I caught the episode of *Gilligan's Island* where a surfer accidentally travels all the way from California to the island. I have never been fond of Gilligan episodes where outsiders come to the island, partly because the outsiders always go back home, and this seems to contradict the fundamental thesis of the show, which I define as "the strandedness." It leaves me feeling uneasy. It's as if I am being asked to believe something that defies logic, in the way that quantum mechanics makes a shambles of Newtonian physics. Whenever low-budget TV makes me ponder physics, I grow uneasy.

I much prefer it when the castaways have to deal with an island-specific plight on their own, such as an active volcano, or cannibals. I don't mind cannibals visiting the island now and then since they come from tribes indigenous to the South Pacific—assuming of course that there really were cannibals inhabiting the Pacific islands in the southern hemisphere between the years 1963–65. I can't imagine why Sherwood Schwartz would risk making up something that could easily be disproven with a bit of anthropological research. Unless he was strapped for a plot.

But here's the thing. As I watched the big dumb blonde surfer boy wander around the island being baffled by his plight, I started thinking about hippies. The island itself was not unlike a hippie commune. Even Gilligan had once been the beatnik Maynard.

As an aside, if you ever want to win a bar bet with an obscure trivia question, ask your friends what the Skipper's real name is, and I don't mean Alan Hale, I mean the fictional character on the show. If you don't know his name, do a bit of research. I would tell you myself but I don't want to spread it around—I rake in more than fifty dollars a month posing that question, just enough to cover my bar tab. Most suckers do say "Alan Hale," and that's when I clean up.

Anyway, the castaways had—accidentally, as the opening song makes crystal clear—gone to this tropic isle and built a functioning society. This had been the goal of all hippie communes in the 1960s. I had never visited a hippie commune, but I had read quite a bit about them in contemporary culture articles as well as R. Crumb comics, and it struck me that the communes of the '60s might have succeeded if only they had included a millionaire and his wife.

The absence of free love and drugs may have contributed to the success of the Gilligan communards, although the presence of Gilligan himself arguably diminished their odds of survival. But think how boring the show would have been without Bob Denver. I'm not naive enough to believe that Hollywood TV scriptwriters are fountainheads of deep philosophical profundity, but I personally think Gilligan was symbolic of something. Let's just leave it at that. Nothing destroys the beauty of a poem faster than parsing it line by line, so you can imagine what it does to sitcoms.

I finally shut off the TV and decided to go to my typewriter. It had been two months since I had last completed an unpublishable manuscript, and I felt that working on something new would take my mind off the Bombalini business.

My unpublishable manuscripts differ somewhat from my uncompleted manuscripts. The uncompleted manuscripts are holdovers from my college days, when I had not yet found the inner fire necessary to finish three hundred pages that had no possibility whatsoever of being accepted by a publisher. I developed that skill after I started cab driving.

My long-range plan, of course, was to write publishable manuscripts. I still remember the pride I felt the first time I ever wrote "The End" on a three-hundred-page manuscript. In college, I used to type "The End" on blank sheets of paper just to see how it felt, and it felt pretty good. I looked forward to doing it for real. Naturally I tore the "The End" sheets to shreds and crumpled them up and hid them in my wastebasket in case any English majors happened to fall by my pad on the way to a bar. This was back in the 3.2 days, when a lot of my Inglés compadres were younger than myself and drank only beer.

A student friend who smoked a pipe once tapped his ashes into my wastebasket and a pile of "The End"s burst into flames. He attempted to smother the flames by slapping at them with his beret, but I grabbed the wastebasket and ran into the bathroom and doused them with water. I don't know if he saw any of the "The End"s, but he gave me funny looks for the rest of the evening. He also did this after reading my short stories. However, I never wrote "The End" at the end of the short stories I handed in to my creative writing classes because that was considered a "commercial" affectation. I don't know what the current philosophy of writing is among young academics nowadays, but back when I was in college the general consensus was that a short story should simply "dangle." By this it was meant that a reader ought to be able to deduce that the story had ended due to the fact that there were no more sentences.

Of course the truth was that I desperately wanted to write "The End" at the end of my short stories because I had every intention of becoming a commercial writer. That was my deepest, darkest secret in college. As far as I know, nobody ever got wind of my secret, including the publishing companies.

Perhaps I was being a bit disingenuous when I said that I had never made any effort in the direction of trying to get rich. By "effort" I simply meant normal-person effort, as opposed to what I do. Scratch tickets, blockbuster bestsellers, and clever inventions describe the landmarks dotting the scenic route I have driven during my efforts to stop doing things forever.

By clever inventions I mean such things as tennis shoes that come in two colors, red for the left foot and green for the right foot. I was once convinced that the teens of America would go for a fashion statement like that, but I hesitated to approach a tennis shoe manufacturer and describe the invention to him because he might steal my idea. In order to sue him I would have to be rich, but in order to be rich I would have to sue him. It was a classic case of *Catch-22,* one of my favorite novels. You can imagine the vexation I felt when *The World According to Garp* was published in paperback books that were sold in different colors. There went my tennis shoes.

I dusted off my Smith-Corona and set it up on my writing table, which is normally my beer table when I am on spring break. Then I dusted off a sheaf of blank paper and found some dusty pencils and a dusty eraser, and began putting myself into the "writer" frame of mind. I do this by closing my eyes and thinking for exactly twenty minutes. I stole this idea from the Maharishi. It's like Transcendental Meditation minus the cosmic consciousness.

Twenty minutes later I didn't have any ideas for a book, but I went ahead and wrote "Chapter 1" on a blank sheet of paper just to kick-start the process. It felt good to be back in the harness.

Then the phone rang.

Infuriated, I sat back and stared at the dusty receiver. As I said, I never answer telephones, not even my own. I waited for it to stop ringing so I could get back to work on my novel, but it just kept ringing. Whenever I hear a telephone ringing on a TV show I turn off the sound. The ringing of a telephone is the most horrific sound on earth. I respond to it the way most people respond to a taximeter. There is something about a ticking taximeter that makes people's skin crawl. In the case of a telephone, it means somebody thinks they know where I am. I would rather sit in the backseat of a Yellow Cab than listen to a telephone, but we all have our crosses to bear.

I counted fifteen rings before I finally capitulated and picked up the receiver. It was Mrs. Bombalini.

"I'm so sorry to bother you, Murph," she said. "I hope I'm not interrupting anything."

I glanced at the dust on my typewriter and almost laughed. "You're not interrupting anything at all, Mrs. Bombalini."

"I was under the impression that you were still driving tonight," she said.

"I quit early, Mrs. Bombalini. I do that sometimes on Sunday," and any other day of the week.

"I called Rocky Cab and they told me you had signed out. I hope you will forgive me, but I lied to them and told them this was an emergency. A man named Rollo gave me your home number."

Rollo!

I filed this info in my Rolodex under R for revenge, although I had mixed feelings. I was, in fact, glad that Mrs. Bombalini had called me at home. It saved me from calling her at home. "That's quite all right," I said. "What's the problem?"

"I think Tony may have gone back to the dog track this evening, and I was going to ask you to go out there and see. After he got home last night I told him that I knew he had been at the track, but he denied it."

Yikes!

"But if you're not working I won't ask you to do this, Murph. I was going to insist that you let me pay you for your time, but I suppose I will just have to go out to the track myself and confront him."

"That's not necessary," someone said. I looked around the apartment. It seemed to be coming from me. "I go to the dog track every Sunday night," the voice lied. "I like to think of Sunday as my real payday. When it comes to picking dogs, I've got a foolproof system. Sunday is dog-day for me." I grabbed my throat and squeezed, but I kept talking. "So if I see Tony out there tonight, I'll let you know."

"Would you? That would be so kind of you. And I want to pay you, Murph. I'll pay you whatever it would have cost if you were driving your taxi."

"Tut tut, I wouldn't hear of it," the voice said. It sounded like William Powell.

"I insist," Myrna Loy replied.

"We can discuss it at another time," I said. I almost added "my dear." I hurried things along. "In fact I was just getting ready to leave for the track. I usually stay until the last race, so it might be late when I call you, unless you want me to call you tomorrow. They don't have public telephones at the dog track, you know."

"I didn't know that."

"Oh yes. It's a standard convention at all the tracks. It keeps the riffraff from cheating," or something.

"Please call me when it's convenient for you, Murph. I appreciate this."

"Think nothing of it," my dear.

We rang off. I went into the bathroom. With a bit of hesitation I looked at my face in the mirror. I was afraid I would see Joanne Woodward, but it was just me. I was grateful to Mrs. Bombalini for calling. I felt as if I was about to truly earn my three bills. I felt as if I was a commercial writer who had hammered "The End" at the bottom of a short story and didn't give a damn who knew it.

I put on my deep forest green Rocky jacket and slapped my Rocky cap onto my head. If Tony Bombalini was at the track, I was going to confront him. He had the sweetest wife in the world and I was going to let him know it, even if it meant bringing Big Al into the picture. The odds were good that Big Al and I would be quits after this night, but I didn't care. I once made a list of all the friends that I had lost since high school, and the list got so long I ran out of paper. But I had plenty of paper now. I ripped "Chapter 1" out of my typewriter and pinned it to my corkboard, where I could get to it later. I paused a moment and stared at my free pass to Putt-Putt. I wondered if Putt-Putt was still in business. I hadn't played miniature golf since I was in the army.

The city was quiet. The streets were empty. I drove north through the darkness hunched forward in my heap, my hands gripping the steering wheel at the ten/two position used by old pros. It wasn't until I got to Vasquez Boulevard that the traffic began picking up. The hop-heads were descending on the Coliseum where dreams were born and died every twenty minutes. At the horse track it takes forty-five minutes between dreams. The track is gigantic. After you've attended a dozen or so horse races, the dog track seems like a Putt-Putt golf course.

The lights of the kennel club came into view, making the residual smog glow overhead. It was like a beacon calling to every loser in the city. I was among them, but I was not of them. I had learned my lesson years ago. As I guided my heap toward the stadium, I tried to make a list of all the lessons I had learned since high school. It filled a yellow sticky note.

The parking lot attendants were guiding cars into slots with a practiced efficiency that you see only in places where Big Money makes the rules, like Las Vegas or Disneyland. I've been to Disneyland. I don't want to talk about it.

I pulled into a slot and got out without bothering to lock my car. If the vermin wanted it, they could have it. They could have my doors anyway. All I cared about was finding Tony. I crossed the vast lot and looked up at the rim of the stadium where little flags were waving in a breeze like little businessmen exhorting customers to make even bigger bets. I couldn't help but feel that Moog was behind all this.

I passed through the turnstile and didn't bother to buy a tip-sheet from a vendor. I wasn't going to hide my face. I was through pretending. Not forever—just with the Bombalini business. I wanted Tony to see me coming. I climbed the stairs to the clubhouse and passed the black security guard, who looked at me funny. I ignored him. I began scanning the crowd, using the thousand-yard stare I had learned in the army. That didn't work, so I cut it down to twenty yards.

I didn't see Tony. I began moving slowly through the throng. I made my way toward the people lined up at the betting windows. If I saw Tony I planned to tackle him before he made a bet, although the security guard was still giving me funny looks. I knew he was giving me funny looks because I kept sneaking peeks at him surreptitiously. I cut that out and focused.

I walked from one end of the clubhouse to the other, scanning each individual, but I didn't see Tony. I began to get the feeling that Mrs. Bombalini's suspicions might be wrong. Maybe Tony wasn't there. Maybe Tony was up in Central City, broadening their tax base. Seventeen hundred bucks could feed a lot of slots.

I stopped walking. When I was in the Boy Scouts they taught us that if we ever got lost in a jungle we should stand still and stay put. That advice obviously came from someone who was never chased by a gorilla. I was near a snack stand so I bought a beer. Imagine drinking beer in a jungle. Alone. Lost. Drunk. I've been there.

Then I heard a voice say, "Your friend is down by the track looking at the dogs."

I turned around and saw Big Al standing behind me.

He was holding a tip-sheet in one hand and a beer in the other. "I was wondering when you would show up," he said.

The sonofabitch could read me like two X-rays. "How long has he been here?" I said.

"Since the first race," Big Al said. "But he hasn't been betting." He took a drink from his cup. "I believe he is waiting for the twin-quin to run." Then he gave me "the look." I was familiar with "the look." He had given it to me during my first and only season at the track years ago, when I had shown up five nights in a row trying to revive the thrill of my eight-hundred-dollar downfall.

"Thanks."

I threw away my beer and made my way through the crowd to the stairwell that descended to the track. A broad asphalt plain slopes gently from the bleachers down to the cyclone fence that separates the track from the crowd. The slope is designed so the people at the rear can have as good a view of the running dogs as the people clinging desperately to the fence. I admired the genius of the design. It was the kind of slope where Big Money designs things. It had Moog written all over it.

I walked down the slope looking around at the crowd, then I went over to the fenced pen where the dogs for the next race were being prepped for their regal strut to the starting gate. Young people in fancy dress jackets were holding leashes and keeping the muzzled dogs calm. Each dog had its own color and number. Tony was right up against the fence staring at the numbers. A tip-sheet was rolled into a tube in one fist.

I walked up behind him. I took a deep breath and said, "Stick with cutting heads."

He froze. I waited.

He slowly turned around and looked at me. "Murph! What are you doing here?"

"I came here to tell you a story," I said. "A story about a young man who once pinned all his hopes and dreams on four dogs and a prayer."

Tony frowned. The frown wasn't as deep as the security guard's frown, but that's because Tony wasn't giving me a frown of derision. It was a frown of uncertainty, whereas the security guard knew exactly what he was dealing with.

Tony glanced at the dogs in the cage. The race wasn't due to start for another ten minutes.

"You'll have to excuse me, Murph," he said. "I need to go place a bet."

"No, you don't," I said. "The only thing you need to do is to listen to me."

The frown was replaced by a look of bafflement.

"I've got a message for you from your wife." I said. "Let's take a walk." I held out my hand as if to grab him by the sleeve.

The bafflement was replaced by something that vaguely resembled fear, the kind of expression you get when everything starts to make too much sense.

He reluctantly moved away from the fence, unrolling the tip-sheet and looking down at it.

"Why don't you toss that into the trash, Tony?" I said. "It beats tossing your money into the trash."

But he didn't. He rolled it back up and held onto it the same way that passengers on the *Titanic* held onto the guard railings, as if their reluctance to let go was relevant.

"Let me buy you a beer," I said.

He nodded but didn't say anything. He looked nervous, and I knew why. The betting windows would be closing in nine minutes. Liquor stores and betting windows inevitably close—and like the security guard, I knew exactly what I was dealing with. I'm third-generation Irish-Catholic.

"When did you talk to my wife?" Tony said as we ascended the stairs to the clubhouse.

I didn't reply. I pointed at a table near a snack stand. Tony took a chair. I went to the stand and bought two plastic cups of draft. When I got back to the table I set one in front of him and sat down.

I raised my cup. "Here's to the women."

Tony reached out and grasped his cup, then he let go and bowed his head. I shrugged and drank mine off. I'm third-generation Irish-Catholic.

"You didn't tell your wife about your big win the other night, did you Tony?" I said.

A curtain of astonishment dropped over his face. "How did you know about that?" he said.

"The dog track is my second home," I lied. "I was standing behind you when you cashed your ticket. You didn't see me. All you saw was that stack of bills the nice lady at the window was shoving across the counter."

He blinked a few times. I could tell by the look in his eyes that he believed me. In my line of work, and in my rear-view mirror, you see a lot of eyes. I know my eyes.

"I've been playing the dogs since I got out of college," I lied. Maybe I'll drop the phrase "I lied" from now on. I'm sure you're familiar enough with my cavalier attitude toward facts to accurately discern when I'm shucking-and-jiving.

"I even asked a friend of mine to write a computer program to help me pick the dogs in the twin-quin, and do you know what?"

"What?" he said, his voice barely a whisper.

"Whenever people asked me how I came out at the end of a season, I would tell them that I broke even. I lied to them, Tony. Nobody breaks even. Not at the dog track and not in life. You either come out ahead, or behind. Mostly behind."

The look of fear came over him again. "But my wife ... when did you talk to her?"

"I first talked to her last Thursday."

I told him everything. By "everything" I mean "almost everything." That's as close to the truth as I normally get.

After I told him that his wife had asked me to follow him to the track, his face became a carousel of colors, then settled on off-white.

"Angelina loves you, Tony," I said. "She's worried about you. She said you have a gambling problem. That's why you're here tonight, isn't it? You figure to parlay that seventeen hundred into eighty-five hundred, don't you? You figure you'll come to the track five nights running and win seventeen hundred every night, right? That's pretty much the way I figured things when I won eight hundred on my first twin. I came to the track every night for a week and do you know what happened?"

He shook his head no.

"I gave my eight hundred back to the nice lady behind the betting window."

Actually I dropped only one hundred dollars before Big Al held his intervention. True story.

"You got lucky the other night and decided that God was on your side, didn't you Tony? You figured you would stick to twin-quins forever. You figured you had plenty of dough to toy with. It's only twenty bucks per bet. You could bet on eighty-five races with seventeen hundred dollars."

My math nuns would have fainted.

"You thought it would be just like going to the bank and withdrawing money every night forever, didn't you Tony? That's what I thought, too. But pretty soon I was dead broke and picking up discarded tickets from the floor, thinking maybe some lucky winner had gotten careless."

Tony looked around at the tickets scattered across the floor. "I've been there, Tony. I know what you're going through. It's hell. Some people call it 'convoluted logic.' Other people call it 'magical thinking.' But just remember this, Tony—God doesn't go to the dog track. He's got His hands full working the foxholes."

Tony closed his eyes and nodded.

He opened them and looked straight at me. "I wanted to make up for all the money I've lost," he said. "When Angelina confronted me the other night and told me she knew I was at the track, I denied it. I lied to her, Murph. But that's because I thought I could make it up to her by bringing home a mountain of cash."

"Angelina doesn't care about cash, Tony. She cares about you."

The warning bell rang. The betting windows would be closing in one minute. Tony looked over at the lines of frantic people leaning toward the windows trying to place last minute bets.

"Heads, Tony," I said. "That's where your money comes from. Damaged follicles. Split ends. Surly teenagers with angry fathers."

He swallowed hard.

"And remember this," I said. "Hair never stops growing." He closed his eyes, took a deep breath, and sighed.

"You're right, Murph. It's just ... it's just that I'm addicted to the rush of gambling. I love betting even more than I love winning."

"I hear you, pal. You're talking to a guy who's been there. Myself, I don't bet the quinellas. Once per season I take a long shot at a trifecta, just to remind myself why I stick with cab driving. I'm a win, place, and show man. Sometimes I almost break even. That's all a man can hope for at the dog track, and in life—a good solid almost."

Tony set the tip-sheet on the table. It unrolled halfway and lay there like a dying cockroach with its legs wavering in the air.

"It's time to leave this place, Tony," I said. "You've got a winner waiting for you at home."

He covered his mouth the way you do to wipe away a milk mustache. Then he tugged at his lapels, got himself together, and stood up. He held out his hand. I shook it.

"Thanks, Murph. You're a good man."

"Keep that under your hat," I said. "Someday I hope to have a reputation to protect."

He let loose and turned away. I watched him break trail through the crowd. As he passed the betting windows the bell rang and the clerks closed the cages. He didn't even glance at them. I waited until he descended the stairs to the parking lot, then I reached across the table, grabbed his beer, and drank it off.

"You done good, Tenderfoot."

I turned in my seat and saw Big Al standing behind me. He moved around to the opposite side of the table and sat down. There was something resembling a twinkle in his eyes. I had never seen Big Al's eyes twinkle before. It disturbed me. He's more of a glare man. "But I ought to sue you for plagiarism," he said. "You had my Save-the-Murph speech down nearly word for word."

I shrugged. "What did you expect?" I said. "I'm an unpublished writer."

CHAPTER 23

When I got back to my crow's nest that night I removed "Chapter 1" from the corkboard, crumpled it up, and tossed it into the trash. I figured it was time to start taking my own advice.

I grabbed a beer from the fridge and carried it into the living room and flopped down in my chair. I picked up my remote control and began surfing. I passed Mary Ann twice before I realized I wasn't even seeing her. I slowly made my way back to the island and stared at it. The beach. The palm trees. The millionaire and his wife. It made me think about Tony and Angelina. Tony was probably home right now telling her everything. By "everything" I mean "everything." And she was probably forgiving him everything. That's what good women do.

I set the remote aside and got up from my chair and crossed the room to the bookshelf. I picked up my copy of *Lolita* and opened it to Chapter 1. I glanced at a paragraph:

"Lo-li-ta: the tip of the tongue taking a trip of three steps down the palate to tap, on three, at the teeth. Lo. Lee. Ta."

That Nabokov. What a Russian.

I took the three hundred dollars out. It didn't feel dirty anymore. It didn't feel like anything at all. It was just money. But it was mine. Until I handed it to the landlord. That's the problem with money. It goes.

I transferred the bills to my *Finnegans*. I didn't bother to count my take for the weekend lease. I knew it would cover my spring break. The problem was that I no longer felt like spreading a beach towel on my living room floor and surrendering myself to a novel with a plot. I should have felt good, but I didn't. I started wondering what the hell I was doing. I had been driving a taxi for fourteen years and writing unpublished novels for twenty years, and all I had to show for it was an acceptance slip from the DOT clinic.

I closed the book and put it away. I went to my typewriter and picked it up and carried it to the closet and put it up on the shelf. Who was I kidding? I didn't know anything about plots. I was never going to be anything but a cab driver. I wondered if Mary Margaret Flaherty had ever forgiven me for wanting to be a writer. I wondered if she had gotten married. I started thinking about giving my Maw a call. Maybe I would ask her about Mary Margaret. But I didn't do it. I didn't want to know. That was one of many things in life I didn't want to know. If I tried to make a list of all the things I didn't want to know, the rain forest would disappear.

I reached for the remote and started to turn off the TV, but a gorilla was chasing Gilligan so I waited until the commercial. It was a commercial for tennis shoes. I turned it off and went into my bedroom. I tried not to look at my Keds as I kicked them under the bed.

I lay in the darkness looking at the view outside the window of my crow's nest. I could see the lights of apartment buildings spread all over Capitol Hill from there, and I knew that inside all of the apartments were hundreds of people, thousands of people, quietly going about their lives. I thought about those people. I saw them every day. They got into my cab and got back out, and I never saw them again. My cab was like Grand Central Station. People coming and going, and except for a few like Tony and Angelina, I never got involved in their personal lives. I stared at the lights in the windows of Capitol Hill, and a thought occurred to me: most of those people were going to die without ever seeing a single one of their dreams realized.

I reached up and pulled down the shade, then yanked the covers over my face and tried to get to sleep. I decided that I would work tomorrow. I had no reason not to. Shoes on the sidewalk, that's the only place where my money was ever going to come from. I was a professional taxicab driver.

I arrived at Rocky Cab around seven the next morning. I walked into the on-call room. Rollo was seated in the cage eating a donut. When he saw me, his eyes got wide and he stopped in mid-chew. I walked up to the window, reached into my pocket, and pulled out seventy dollars.

"Give me a trip-sheet and the keys to one twenty-seven," I said.

"Murph?" Rollo said nervously. "You're working today?"

"You heard me."

"But you just pulled a weekend lease," he said, fumbling with a blank stack of trip-sheets.

"And now I'm pulling a daily lease," I said, counting out the bills and shoving them across the counter.

He was flustered. That was the extent of my revenge. Cab driving was my bread and butter, and one thing I had learned in life, in love, and in the army, was never to hoist yourself on your own petard. There are plenty of other petards to choose from. Yanking Rollo's petard was as close to humiliating him as I could get without putting my job in jeopardy. It's true that I could have gotten a job at one of the other cab companies. A lot of drivers do that, moving from Rocky to Yellow to the other companies and back to Rocky again. On the street it's called "ping-pong." But what's the point? Every cab company has its own Rollo. I didn't want to go to the trouble of learning a new Rollo. I had smaller fish to fry.

I took my key and trip-sheet and walked toward the door, leaving Rollo fingering the fragments of the donut that had crumbled in his nervous fingers. I removed the card that I had filed under R for revenge and tossed it into the trash. I was back to square one. It was Monday morning, and there were shoes on the sidewalk.

I stopped at a 7-11 and filled up on gas, joe, and three packs of Twinkies. You heard me right. Plurals. I used to limit myself to one pack of Twinkies a day, but I used to do a lot of things. I cruised to the Brown Palace and got in line behind four cabs. I shut everything down, picked up my paperback, sipped at my joe, nibbled at a Twinkie, and waited for the pitter-patter of the first hailstones of the morning. The rush hour was still half an hour off, but already the early risers and eager beavers were guiding their sedans along the streets of Denver, trying to beat the rush. It was a fool's ploy. They weren't going anywhere except to work. That's why I stayed in college for seven years. After you graduate from college there's nothing left to do but get a job, and why would anybody rush to do that?

The cab line moved every five minutes. Pretty soon I was first in line. I set my paperback down and looked at myself in the rear-view mirror. I checked my shag and my teeth. There wasn't much I could do about my shag, but I pulled some first-echelon maintenance on my teeth. I took a toothpick out of my briefcase and went to work removing excess Twinkie. As the top brass at Rocky constantly reminded us, good hygiene translated into good tips. Not that there's any other kind of tip. A nickel is a good tip in a bastion of true free enterprise. But cab drivers tend to get spoiled. I'll admit it. It's happened to me. You stumble into a job where people throw free money at you, and pretty soon you start thinking you're entitled to it. But nobody is entitled to a tip. It's just a social custom. God knows who invented it, but I guarantee you it wasn't Moog.

If you happen to be a young male, let me give you a tip. If you really want to impress a cab driver, a dollar is an acceptable gratuity, although why anybody would want to impress a cab driver is beyond me. I do realize that not all young males have a lot of money to throw around, and the idea of giving away cash might feel like a total rip job—but remember: it's good training for April 15. If you don't understand what I mean by April 15, just go out and get a job. You'll find out the hard way.

My left rear door opened and a pedestrian leaned in. "I just missed my bus!" he said. He was young. He was male. He was sweating bullets. "Can you drive me down to Eleventh and Broadway?"

I nodded and started my engine. I had left the locks on my rear doors unlocked on purpose. The idea of being branded by my fellow cabbies hadn't really bothered me, since it would have caused more people to not speak to me for the rest of my life. But I was a professional cab driver and pedestrians come with the territory. A self-help guru would call this attitude "bending with the wind," but I just call it "giving up."

On the trip down to Eleventh he told me he was starting his first day of work ever. He looked eighteen years old. He was panic-stricken. I told him not to worry. I said we would probably even pass his bus before we got to his place of business. I may have been telling the truth, hard to say, but I didn't pay much attention to the bus traffic. Buses and taxis are like jungle animals that sip from the same watering hole—they tolerate each other's presence, then go about their nasty, brutish, and short lives. When we got to Eleventh and Broadway, the fare came three dollars and sixty cents. He handed me a twenty.

"Do you have anything smaller?" I said, bending with the wind.

"No, that's all I have," he said, his eyes wide with panic. This may have been the very first taxi ride of his entire life. I smiled and reached into my shirt pocket and pulled out all of my starting cash. I made a slow show of counting out my fives and ones, then I plucked some nickels from my briefcase and fed them into his palm like birdseed until I had given him sixteen dollars and forty cents in change. I sat back and idly waited to see if he would give me a tip.

I won't bore you with the results.

I sighed and headed back toward the Brown Palace, making a stop at a 7-11 on Lincoln Boulevard for more joe and another Twinkie. When I handed the clerk the twenty, he gave me a funny look. The clerk's name was Fred. He was a former Rocky Cab driver. I explained about the new pair of shoes on the street. He nodded with understanding, then gave me some fresh starting change. He threw the joe in for free, but charged me for the Twinkie. He worked for a corporation now. A security camera was aimed right at his cash register.

When I got back to the Brown there were six cabs in line. I turned my wheels toward the Fairmont. By now the rush hour was in full swing. It was a typical taxi Monday.

As I pulled into line at the Fairmont, a call came over the radio. "One twenty-seven, you've got a personal in east Denver." He gave me the address: Gino's Barbershop.

I sat there with the microphone in my hand but didn't say anything.

"One twenty-seven, do you check?" the dispatcher said. I pressed the button and said, "Check."

"Come on, Murph, stay on the ball," the dispatcher said. "What are you doing working eight days in a row anyway?" It was a rhetorical question. He sailed off into the world of further bells. I hung my mike on the dash.

I placed my hand over my mouth the way you would to wipe away a milk mustache. I just sat there staring out the front window. I began to feel the way I once felt after meeting a woman named Yvette at a New Year's Eve party. We dated a few times, then I stopped calling her. Pretty soon she began calling me. I'm not going to tell you that story, although *Play Misty For Me* touches on the highlights.

I thought about finding a phone booth and just calling Gino's to see what Tony wanted. I doubted it was a ride. The Bombalinis didn't seem to take normal-person rides. I hadn't called Mrs. Bombalini back because I had assumed it wasn't necessary after my intervention with Tony at the track. I hadn't wanted to interrupt their reconciliation conversation, or anything else they might have been doing in the privacy of their home. But maybe I was wrong about that. I'm usually pretty careful about assumptions. You know the drill. But that one had seemed like a sure thing. Now I felt a mild sense of regret. I felt I ought to have gone ahead and called her, just to cross the last tee and dot the last eye. If I had done that I might not have been sitting in line at the Fairmont with my hand over my mouth—clean break, if you get my drift.

Oh well.

I started my engine and pulled out of line and made my way over to Colfax. I thought about driving slowly. Sometimes a fare will call all the taxi companies, and whoever gets there first will get the trip—in theory. If three cabbies show up at the house at the exact same time, there is potential for a mild fracas. But sometimes the drivers will conspire to leave without anyone picking up the fare, leaving the customer high and dry. A multiple-call is a lousy trick to play on cab drivers. The first time I experienced the shotgun approach to calling taxis, I was dumb enough to think the customer had made an error. Big Al set me straight. But the tactic impressed me in a twisted sort of way. I've often wondered how I might apply it in my own life. But the odds of myself finding any practical use for a twisted tactic are slim, since I never do anything.

I decided there was no point in going slowly. I knew Tony wouldn't be calling anybody else. He had requested my personal service. I stepped on the accelerator and switched into the professional mode, getting into the groove, finding The Zone, trying to time the green lights all the way past Monaco Parkway. I wanted to get this over with as quickly as possible.

CHAPTER 24

Then I was there.

Gino's Barbershop sat simmering on a sun-blasted sidewalk of east Colfax, the gateway to Aurora, the enchanted suburb. I pulled up at the curb and looked at the OPEN sign on the door. It looked like a good sign, but what did I know? I used to bet greyhounds based on the resonance of their names. The big dog always won.

I waited to see if Tony might come outside. When he didn't, I took a deep breath and let it out slowly. How many times in my life had I taken a deep breath? Well ... how many times had I done something I didn't want to do? I got out of my cab and walked up to the door, shoved it open, and stepped inside. Gino was sweeping the floor. He glanced at me with his eyebrows raised. I closed the door behind me. Gino leaned the broom against the wall and came toward me with his arms out. "Murph," he said soundlessly. I had seen all the Godfather movies except the third one, so I knew he was going to embrace me ... but the question was why? As the aroma of Butch Wax engulfed me, I glanced around the shop for a dead fish lying on a newspaper.

He got it over with quickly. When he stood back there was a sheen of moisture in his eyes. "Murph," he said aloud. "Angelina told me everything. So I asked you to come here because I wanted to thank you personally for what you did for my Tony." He raised one hand with the palm outward, not unlike a Boy Scout reciting The Oath. "And don't you worry none, Murph, I am going to pay you for your time."

I bent with the wind, and nodded. I had my fill of turning down free money.

"So you're the one who called me here?" I said.

"That's right. Tony ... he's not here. He took the afternoon off." I nodded, then I wondered if that's all Gino wanted. His promise to pay me for my time suddenly didn't sound like such a big deal.

"Tony told me everything, too," Gino said. He turned and strolled over to one of the barber chairs. "Murph, my friend, I want you to take a seat."

I swallowed hard and just stood there.

"Tony told me he promised you a free haircut," Gino said. "I want to give you that free haircut myself. And I'm going to pay you for your time, don't you worry none."

I reached up and felt my shag. We had been through a lot together. Unemployment. Cab driving. That about covered it. I wasn't sure I was ready for such a big change in my life. And Gino didn't look like a man who knew all that much about contemporary fashion statements. I suddenly saw myself as a ten-year-old kid walking out of a barbershop in Wichita, Kansas, looking like Andy Hardy. Mickey Rooney fascinates me, but not that much.

Gino picked up a white apron and gave it a flap, then squinted at me. "Ponytail," he said.

"What?" I said.

"I see you in a ponytail. You remind me of my brother Luigi. Back in the '60s he wore his hair in a ponytail. He was a hippie. He was the black sheep of the Bombalini family. But speaking objectively as a barber, I have to say that he looked good. Not every man can wear a ponytail. But you, Murph, you drive a taxi, you wear a T-shirt, you wear blue jeans, you wear tennis shoes. If the great Michelangelo himself had painted your portrait, he would have given you a ponytail."

I may have been an English major, but I was a sucker for fifteenth-century Italian Renaissance analogies.

I walked over to the barber chair and took a seat on the slippery upholstery. It felt strange. I hadn't sat on an old-fashioned barber chair since the day before I got my discharge from the army. My sergeant made me do it.

I didn't really want to kiss my shag goodbye. I had already kissed my bad eyesight goodbye, and the glasses turned out to be a pain in the neck. I've never liked extraneous motion in general, and having to put my glasses on just to watch cable was as annoying as brushing my teeth—and you know how I feel about tying my shoes.

I took off my glasses, closed my eyes, and prayed. Gino went to work.

"Maybe you're wondering where my Tony is right now, eh?" Gino said.

I started to nod, then stopped. I had forgotten about the proper protocol for undergoing a haircut. One slip of the clip and you're wearing your hat indoors for two weeks.

"Yes," I said.

"He's with Angelina," he said. "She came by to pick him up. He'll be back later. Right now they're talking to a man who runs a Gamblers Anonymous group in Aurora."

"I'm glad to hear that, Mr. Bombalini."

"Call me Gino,"

"Okay ... Gino."

Ten minutes later I was looking at the back of my head in a small mirror held up by Gino. It looked good. My hair was still long but lacked the familiar stamp of my amateur efforts. Some people call it "good grooming."

Gino gave my neck a final brush with the whisk broom, then yanked the apron off my torso with the flair of Hemingway performing a veronica. He went to the cash register and punched a button. The cash drawer slid out and he started plucking bills from the box.

He turned to me and held up an open palm. "No arguments," he said with his head cocked at an angle. "Today the barber pays the customer."

I bent. He paid.

He paid well.

I tucked the bills into my pocket and thanked him for the cut. "There is something else I want to do for you, Murph," Gino said.

Strangely, this was like a knife in my heart. I hate it when people offer to "do" something for me because it inevitably involves my doing something that I don't want to do, like go somewhere I've never been before, or spend money on "a really good deal!!!"

"I own a restaurant a few blocks east of here called Bombalini's," Gino said. "And I want you to know that as long as you live, you may eat your meals free in my restaurant. You will never pay."

That was a straight line so dangerous that I started mentally doing the times tables. Elvis Presley taught me that. Not in person, but in *Follow That Dream,* my favorite Elvis movie based on a novel. My second favorite Elvis movie based on a novel is *King Creole.* That novel was *A Stone for Danny Fisher* written by—of all people—Harold Robbins. I once checked into it and Elvis does not appear anywhere in the book. I suspect that there were massive rewrites in the screenplay, although I have no proof—yet.

"Any time you want a free spaghetti dinner, you come to Bombalini's," Gino said. "I will introduce you to my nieces and nephews who work as waiters and waitresses."

"I'll be sure to do that," I said, uncertain as to whether or not I was lying. I often promise to do things that I have no intention of doing just so my benefactors will go away. But I was intrigued by the magic word "free."

Gino then told me that he didn't expect Tony to be back from GA for another hour. I said I would like to stick around just to say hi to Tony, but I had some personal business that I needed to attend to right away. I told him I would drop by the shop later in the week to let Tony see my new head. Gino smiled broadly and nodded.

I left the shop and climbed into 127, took a moment to adjust the cap strap for my new hair, then started the engine. I glanced into the rear-view mirror as I drove away and saw Gino standing in the doorway. He was beaming. You don't see a lot of beaming in my line of work. It felt good.

Even though I hate going to places I've never been to before, I decided to make a run past Bombalini's just to get the lay of the land. That's what I told myself anyway. But deep down inside I knew that the word "free" had destroyed my free will. I drove east until I saw the place, a cozy little bistro not far from Fitzsimmons Army Hospital where President Eisenhower had recovered from his heart attack during the 1950s. I wondered if the Russkies had contemplated attacking America while the president was laid up. To my knowledge, they didn't attack, but it occurred to me that Richard Nixon must have liked being substitute president for a short while there. I don't want to get political here, but this reminded me of the episode of *The Andy Griffith Show* when Barney Fife was made sheriff for the day while Andy was away on business. Barney jailed half the town, including the mayor and Aunt Bea. Even Opie got swept up in the dragnet! It was not only a rib-tickling knee-slapper, in some ways it foreshadowed the '60s, but let's not get into that.

Rather than live a lie as usual, I nodded and told myself that I would go to Bombalini's as soon as I could, partly to please Gino, but mostly to prevent my invisible Maw from snarling, "It's free, fer the luvva Christ!"

Then I turned my thoughts to the personal business I wanted to attend to. It had to do with extraneous motion. The plan had come to me as I was sitting in Gino's barber chair, staring at my unfocused mug in the wall mirror. I drove straight west until I hit Broadway, then I turned south toward the intersection of Alameda. I was headed for a cozy little dive called SightCity!!! I wanted to check on something a woman once said to me, something I almost missed because I was too balled up in my ego to see The Big Picture, something to do with an invention called "disposable contacts." On sale.

To make a longer story shorter, nowadays when I open my eyes at dawn I'm already prepped to seize the day. No more fumbling for scratched-up specs. I bought the kind of contacts you can wear in your sleep. The only drawback is that the landscapes of my dreams aren't as surreal as they used to be. But I'm so pleased with my contact lenses that I'm seriously thinking about having a dentist remove all of my teeth. No more brushing. Just pop in a set of plastic choppers at dawn and hit the road—but I'm going to give that a little more thought.

I did see Tony later that week. He's "off the dog" as they say in GA. Gambling is one of the few vices that flesh is heir to that never got its hooks into me. My little fling with the twin-quin years ago was an anomaly, a fool's ploy that had more to do with bad addition than addiction. The nuns wouldn't have been surprised. I've passed through Reno on a number of occasions since then, but I've never stopped because there is just something about giving free money to men in black vests that makes my skin crawl. As for scratch tickets ... well ... all cab drivers have to buy a minimum of one scratch ticket per week. PUC regulation.

After I got off work that Monday night I made a quick run to the grocery store to get The Big Grind out of the way. There were a lot of customers in the store with a lot of full carts. As I plucked cans and meat products off the shelves, I kept count until I had to give up on my hope of making it through the ten-items-or-less line. That's a mind game I play every week, and I always lose. When my cart was full I headed for the checkout stands, eyeing the little old ladies with their dreaded change purses. I'm not all that familiar with European military history, but I suspect there was a little old lady in front of Napoleon at Waterloo.

And then, just as I was lethargically wheeling my shopping cart toward a long line, I heard a voice say, "I can help somebody over here." A cash register was opening up in front of me. Mon Dieu!

I began unloading my food onto the conveyor belt. A clatter of wheels arose at my back. Shopping carts were racing toward the register like an L-5 at the Brown, but I was first in line. It felt so good that I took my time giving the cashier exact change.

When I got home I grabbed a beer from the fridge and went into the living room and sat down. I stared at the blank face of the TV for a moment. I was still feeling good. This was a bad sign. Prior to that week, feeling good often led me to my typewriter. Even if I didn't have a plot in mind, feeling good made me want to wrestle with the Play-Doh of language. But that was all over. Twenty years of getting nowhere had finally taught me the one lesson about writing that I hadn't expected to learn: quit.

They didn't teach that in the how-to books.

I got up and went to my cigar box and pulled out a stogie. I normally smoke cigars only at Sweeney's Tavern, or when writing, but I felt that this might fill the void created by the new reality. I lit up and took a few puffs, but it only made me think about adjectives. I stubbed it out. I realized that I had something in common with Tony. Giving up writing would be as difficult as giving up gambling. Both activities comprise something you do because you think it will take you some place else, some place you've always dreamed of being. Only you never get there because there's always one more dog race, one more slot machine, one more adjective. And when you know less about grammar than you know about arithmetic, it's time to face the music.

I started thinking about writing a book called "Face The Music, Chump." It would be a gut-wrenching tale of rejection slips. Yeah, I did have a lot in common with Tony. I wondered if there was a place where a guy like me could get rid of the craving to scribble. Some kind of Writers Anonymous, although most writers are anonymous. A place where human wreckage with Smith-Coronas could gather to cure themselves of hanging around office supply stores while their kids starved. I needed a twelve step program and I needed it bad. Step #1: admit you have a plotting problem.

But I couldn't see myself getting up in front of a crowd of strangers and saying, "Hi. My name is Murph."

It made my skin crawl.

The general consensus was that an addict can't go it alone, but I was going to give it a try, i.e., try to quit thinking about earning money off novels. Money can't buy happiness——but it can buy beer. I picked up my beer and took a sip, then I picked up my remote and switched on the cable. I set sail for *Gilligan's Island*. Pretty soon I was watching Ginger and Mary Ann frolic on a jerrybuilt theater stage alongside Phil Silvers. It was the infamous Hamlet musical. The dream of all islanders like myself, of course, is to catch Hans Conried in his classic portrayal of Wrongway Feldman, the marooned WWI flying ace. Even Mary Ann fades into the background when the host of Fractured Flickers steps into the limelight. And dig this: there were two Wrongway Feldman episodes, and both of them were directed by Ida Lupino.

But something started nagging at me. I could barely keep my eyes on the girl from Winfield. I continued to watch until Sgt. Bilko figured out a way to swindle the castaways and make a big comeback on Broadway. Then I turned off the TV because I realized what was nagging at me. Who was I trying to kid? I knew everything about plots. I had seen every TV show broadcast since 1955. I could recite from memory the plot of every *Andy of Mayberry, Leave it to Beaver, The Dick van Dyke Show,* and yes—*My Mother the Car.*

I saw the light that night.

Seven years of college had dimmed the bulbs of my creativity, but now they were blazing at sixty watts. I got out of my chair and went to my closet. I reached up and grabbed my dusty typewriter and carried it over to my beer table. I realized that, as an English major, I had been looking for plots in all the wrong writers. Hemingway? I never saw one of his characters put on a gorilla costume and chase a skirt around the Eiffel Tower. And Faulkner? He had the jokes if you had the bowie knife sharp enough to hack his language down to the punch lines. But the answer to my writing problems had been staring me in the eye ever since me ol' Dad bought a Motorola.

I forgot all about dying without ever seeing a single one of my dreams realized. I set up shop at my writing table and dusted off my sheaf.

I closed my eyes and thought for exactly twenty minutes, and when I raised my eyelids I had my story nailed down. I even had the title: "Deliverance 2: Kentucky Kayaks." It's twenty years later and the sons of the original characters are riding the whitewater, looking for hillbillies.

I set to work typing "Chapter 1" believing with all my heart that the final manuscript would never stand the slightest chance of ever being published.

It felt good to be back in the harness.

THE END

TICKET TO HOLLYWOOD

BOOK 2 IN
THE ASPHALT WARRIOR SERIES

Coming Soon!

CHAPTER 1

I had just dropped off a fare at a bar on east Colfax when a call came over the radio for an address on Capitol Hill. The customer wanted to go to Larimer Square. I snatched the microphone off the dash and said, "One twenty-seven." With luck I might make five more bucks before quitting time. It was winter, it was dark, and I wanted to go home, but I took the call because driving a cab is like playing a slot machine: when you win, you win money.

The dispatcher gave me an address for an apartment building on 14th Avenue. I had picked up fares there before. Young people. Students. Punks. Losers. Unemployed. My kind of people. As soon as I pulled up at the curb, the foyer door opened and a young woman came out dressed like a flapper. It didn't take F. Scott Fitzgerald to tell me where she was going: the Mile-Hi Film Festival. Bigwigs from Hollywood always attended the festival. I was looking forward to having a bigwig in the backseat of my taxi, but bigwigs rode in limousines. I didn't blame them. If I was a bigwig I would go first class, too. But realistically speaking, the odds of me ever becoming a bigwig are six-to-one.

As soon as she climbed into the backseat I smelled vodka. During the brief moment that the overhead light was on, I noted that my fare was probably eighteen, but the dress made her look nineteen. It was white, tight, and short. She was wearing a flapper cap. She was clutching a beaded purse. Strings of pearls were draped around her neck. She threw herself into a reclining position and leaned her head against the far door and said, "I want to go to ... you know ... that place downtown."

Smirnoff Vodka, if I wasn't mistaken, and I usually wasn't.

"The Flicker?" I said.

A wide smile elbowed its way between her cheeks. "How did you know?" she said.

I knew because that's where *The Great Gatsby* was showing. I had browsed through the film festival schedule over the weekend, making red checkmarks next to the movies I didn't want to see.

"A lucky guess," I said. "You look like Zelda Fitzgerald."

"Who?" she said.

I dropped my flag and pulled away from the curb. I had the feeling this was going to be a long five minutes.

"She was a flapper," I said. "She was married to the guy who wrote *The Great Gatsby.*"

"Don't you just love that movie?" she said.

"Love ain't the word."

"I've seen it fourteen times," she said

"That's a lot of times to see a movie," I said. "Did you ever read the book?"

"What book?"

I swallowed hard.

"*The Great Gatsby,*" I said. "It's a novel."

"Really?" she said. "I've never read a novel. I'm an actress."

I opened my mouth to say something, but nothing came out. In my entire life I had never heard two sentences like that uttered consecutively. We rode in silence for a bit, then I heard her moving in the backseat. She was sitting up. I looked at the rear-view mirror and saw her leaning toward the front seat. She rested her arms on the seatback.

"Do you know him?" she said.

"Know who?"

"The guy who wrote that book."

"He died a long time ago."

"Oh," she said. "I thought maybe you were friends with him."

I was wrong. It was Gilbey's, not Smirnoff. I suddenly realized she was carrying a half-pint in her purse. I realized it when she pulled it out and held it in front of my nose.

"Want a drinkie?" she said.

I raised my hand and eased the bottle out of my line of vision. I'm a beer man. "Aren't you a little young to be drinking vodka?"

She pouted and flopped back against the seat. "You sound like my faaaaather," she said. She unscrewed the cap and took a snort.

This made me feel bad. It reminded me of college. But that was long ago and in another time zone.

We came to Lincoln Boulevard. I made a right turn toward midtown. I glanced at her in the mirror and said, "It's kind of cold out. Don't you have a coat?"

She took another drink and put the booze away. "I don't need a coat where I'm going."

"Where are you going?"

"To a party. They're having a costume party after the movie."

I had the urge to counter her logic, but I was talking to a drunk person. I had wended my way through conversations with plenty of drunks before, but never one this young, at least not as a cab driver. College is another story. "Are you meeting friends there?" I said.

She started giggling. "Yes, daddy, I'm meeting friends there."

"Are they actors, too?" I said.

She frowned at me. "Why do you keep asking me so many quesssstions?"

I ran her tone of voice and facial expression through the Univac inside my brain. It spit out a card that said ease off. Her life was none of my business. My rule-of-thumb is to never get involved in the personal lives of my fares. My success rate is about as big as my thumb.

"Just making conversation," I said. "Acting interests me. Driving a cab is sort of like being an actor. And I had friends in college who were actors. I know a lot of people who aren't what they seem to be."

"You went to college?" she said.

"I graduated fifteen years ago," I said.

"Did you major in cab driving?" she said, and burst out laughing.

I'll admit it. She zinged me. I filed her quip in my mental Rolodex under P for plagiarism. I know a keeper when I hear one.

I grinned and said, "Nah, I was an English major."

"Is that how come you know so much about books?" she said.

"That's how come," I replied.

I slowed for the light at 18th Avenue. The Flicker was a small art theater in Larimer Square at 15th. I was forced by downtown Denver's spectacular one-way street system to circle three blocks out of my way and come at it from the north. They were showing a lot of F. Scott Fitzgerald movies at The Flicker that week. God knows why. Maybe because Hemingway refused to write screenplays. William Faulkner didn't refuse though. He sold out plenty of times. That's one of the two things I like most about Faulkner. The other is Flem Snopes.

"Your ponytail is cute," she said.

"Thanks."

"Are you a hippie?"

"No."

"You look like a hippie."

"That's part of my act. Like I always say, there's no business like show business except cab driving. Role-playing is crucial. If I looked like the kind of person I really am, I would never get tips."

"I love acting."

"What kind of acting do you do?"

"I had the lead role in my high school play."

"Yeah? What play was that?"

"*Carousel.*"

"*Carousel,*" I said. I didn't know what else to say.

"I sang in it," she said.

"Are you a good singer?"

"I am a very good singer," she said. "My teacher told me so. Mr. Delrubio said I should be on Broadway."

I thought about this as The Flicker came into view. The world is full of Mr. Delrubios. I have a few Delrubios tucked away in a steamer trunk in my apartment. But I decided not to comment on Mr. Delrubio. Having never met the guy personally, I did not feel it appropriate to pass judgment on what I naturally assumed was bad advice. I assume all advice is bad, even my own.

I stopped at the red light at 15th and Larimer, and suddenly the girl in the backseat started singing. She sang very quietly and very melodiously: "... Off you will go in the mist of day, never ever to know, how I loved you ..." and she stopped.

I waited for her to sing "... soooo ..." but she didn't.

It wasn't until sometime later that I learned that Rogers and Hammerstein hadn't given that lyric a so.

The light turned green. I pulled the cab forward and parked at the curb outside The Flicker. There was a crowd of people waiting in line to get into the movie. "Six-forty," I said, pointing directly at my taximeter.

The girl leaned forward and squinted at the meter. Then she reached down the front of her dress and pulled out a ten-dollar bill and handed it to me.

"Keep the change, Charley," she said with giggle.

"Thanks," I said.

She opened the door and got out, closed it, and walked toward the throng waiting to see Robert Redford's portrayal of Scott Fitzgerald's gold-hatted high-bouncing lover. I waited to see if anyone stepped forward to greet her, but she melded with the crowd and disappeared.

She was a just a kid, and I had a feeling she didn't belong where she was going, but that's true of most people. A horn honked. I looked at my rear-view mirror. A Yellow Cab was waiting to get into my space at the curb. The driver had a whole slew of gold-hatted high-bouncers in his hack. I took one last look at the throng on the sidewalk, then I put my cab into gear and pulled away from the curb.

If it hadn't been so close to the end of my shift, I would have cruised along Larimer Square looking to pick up a pedestrian or two. Normally I don't deal with pedestrians hailing cabs on the street. Denver isn't like New York City where people are always flagging taxis and riding eight blocks. I don't know how the cabbies in New York City make it. I've never been to New York. Whenever I see a movie set in New York, the streets look like a river of Yellow Cabs. Before I started driving a cab, I had never taken notice of them on the streets of Denver, but after I got my license I started seeing taxis everywhere. The competition looked stiff. I hate competition. It's one of the seven warning signs of work. I've spent most of my life trying to figure out ways to make money without working. I don't know what I could do to get money besides driving a cab, except robbing banks. Both occupations have their pros and cons. For instance, bank robbery isn't quite as dangerous as cab driving, but it pays better.

I made my way back over to Broadway, leaving the glitz and glamour of Hollywood behind me. As much as I tried not to, I hoped the girl would be okay. As I said, I avoid getting involved in the personal lives of my fares. As a professional cab driver it is incumbent upon me to treat my customers the same way a doctor treats his patients: keep them alive long enough to get the money.

But I started thinking about *The Great Gatsby*. I first read it when I was a junior at the University of Colorado at Denver, which is, ironically, three blocks away from The Flicker. It's an urban school spread over a few blocks of downtown. *Gatsby* was assigned to my English class, but on the day we were due to discuss it, the teacher found out that practically nobody had read the book. Nobody seemed to understand the symbolism of the green light at the end of Daisy's dock.

The teacher went down the rows of desks asking each student if he or she had read the book. Everyone said no. Everyone except me. I felt like a traitor. An outsider. An egghead. Fortunately I didn't understand the symbolism either, but I still felt like a pariah.

But I couldn't stop thinking about the actress who had told me she had never read a novel. Who was I to judge her? She was like an English major, the poor kid. I put her out of my mind and drove back toward the Rocky Mountain Taxicab Company (RMTC). It was quitting time. My fake weekend had begun. I always take Tuesday off, unless my rent is due and I need to pick up some extra cash. I always take Thursday off, too. I have two fake weekends and one real weekend per week. Sometimes I wish there were eight days in a week just so I could squeeze in an extra weekend. But we all have our crosses to bear.